Small Scale Quiltmaking

Quiltmaking

Precision, Proportion, and Detail

SMALL SCALE
QUILTMAKING

Precision, Proportion, and Detail

Sally Collins

C&T PUBLISHING

Copyright © 1996 Sally Collins
Developmental editor: Joyce Engels Lytle
Copy editor: Judith M. Moretz
Technical editors: Joyce Engels Lytle and Diana Roberts
Photography: Sharon Risedorph, San Francisco, California
Book Design: Rose Sheifer Graphic Productions, Walnut Creek, California
Illustrations: Ginny Coull, Walnut Creek, California
Cover Design: Irene Morris Design, Monterey, California

Library of Congress Cataloging-in-Publication Data
Collins, Sally
    Small scale quiltmaking : precision, proportion, and detail / Sally Collins.
       p. cm.
    Includes bibliographical references.
    ISBN 1-57120-009-6
    1. Patchwork—Patterns. 2. Quilting. 3. Appliqué. 4. Miniature quilts. I. Title.
TT835.C6474   1996
746.46'0228—dc20   95-46104

We have made every attempt to properly credit the trademark and brand names of
the items mentioned in this book. We apologize to any companies that have been
listed incorrectly, and we would appreciate hearing from you.
Bias Bars is a trademark of Celtic Design Co.
Bias Square is a registered trademark of That Patchwork Place.
Gütermann Quilting Thread is a product of Gütermann & Co.
Hot Tape is a trademark of Distlefink Designs, Inc.
Mettler is a brand name of Arova Mettler AG.
Miniature Medley, Miniature Spectrum©, Miniature Coordinates are fabric
collections of RJR Fashion Fabrics.
Omnigrid is a registered trademark of Onmigrid, Inc.
Quilters GluTube is a registered trademark manufactured by Mark-Tex
exclusively for Quilting Techniques, Inc.
Schmetz is a brand name of Ferd. Schmetz GmbH., Germany.

RJR Fashion Fabrics and Jinny Beyer have recognized and responded to the
need to create proportionately smaller scaled printed fabric to give miniature and
small scale quilts variety, detail, and integrity. The *Mosaic Mask* quilt is made entirely
from the Miniature Medley fabric collection designed by Jinny Beyer for RJR. They
have since printed Miniature Spectrum© and Miniature Coordinates. Sally offers her
sincere thanks to that company and quilt artist for these wonderful fabrics.

Published by C&T Publishing
P.O. Box 1456
Lafayette, California 94549

Printed in Hong Kong
10 9 8 7 6 5 4 3 2 1

TABLE OF CONTENTS

DEDICATION

To my friend and husband, Joe, who is my light, my anchor, my mirror.
Thank you for your unconditional love, support, and honesty.

ACKNOWLEDGMENTS

So many people have helped, contributed, supported, shared, advised, encouraged and loved me throughout this process. To Joe, Sean, and Evelyn for believing in me; to Joyce Lytle, Diana Roberts, and Diane Pedersen of C&T for their expertise and calming influence; to my friend, Glorianne Garza, for always being there to listen; to Sheila Pedersen, Gai Perry, and Claire Jarratt for sharing their treasures; to Sharyn Craig and Joen Wolfrom for their professional advice and encouragement; to Sharon Risedorph for her beautiful pictures; and to Charlene Dakin, Mike Call, Freddy Moran, Janey Edwards, Corrine Pratt, Georgene Smith, Anne Haynes, Trudy Smith, and Cheron Adrian for their unconditional support; thank you with all my heart.

SPECIAL THANKS

I knew absolutely nothing about sewing or quilts when I took my first quiltmaking class in 1978 from Mary Brewer. Mary patiently and gently nurtured my enthusiasm for the quiltmaking process. At the same time, she wisely taught me to respect the traditions of the piecemakers, and to always remember the importance and pleasure of accurate workmanship. As one of many quilters whom Mary has introduced to the process over her years of teaching, I am grateful for the opportunity to say thank you, Mary. The door you so graciously opened for me set me upon a path that has been filled with peace, happiness, and love. If dreams come true, I hope to be able to give as much to each student I meet along the path as you so generously gave to me.

Stepping Out, 45" square

FOREWORD

I was first drawn to quiltmaking in 1978. Quilts stirred warm feelings of family, home, and love within me. A door was opened for me, and I set out upon a path that has led me to joyous fellowship, inner peace, and pure happiness.

Quilts reflect a lot about who we are. While they challenge our minds, our hands, our patience, and our endurance, they give us an outlet for expressing our individual creativity. Quilting teaches us about ourselves, and how we relate to others, in this constantly changing world. The finished quilts represent ageless values we all identify with. They have withstood the many tests of time, and remain symbols of the truth we seek.

Quilting has helped me to better understand tradition, friendship, accomplishment, creativity, and the importance of attending to the details of life. These are lessons well worth learning. The many wonderful people I have met along this path have touched my heart and life in meaningful ways, always leaving so much more than I can ever give in return. The excitement of creating something beautiful, the peacefulness that comes with "putting in the stitch," is what I wish for all who find this work. For me, this book is an opportunity to share what I have learned — one more, of so many, special gifts that have come to me through quiltmaking. Threads of common experience and understanding are woven into a love for quiltmaking. For me, they provide a bridge for connecting with quilters of the past and future. This simple process has given so much, to so many, for a long time. It asks so little in return that I cannot help occasionally being overwhelmed by the beauty of its simplicity.

Through the quiltmaking process I have discovered the wonderful feeling that comes from doing my personal best. Each of us has our own standard of quality, our own unique perspective and experience. That diversity is what makes life and our world of quilting as interesting, as rich, and as colorful as it is. As a teacher, I try to help my students define and achieve their own personal best. From that perspective, I see the "process" of quiltmaking being as important as the finished quilt. It is within the process that we experience those threads that join us all to the past, the future, and to each other. This joining, when all sense of time is lost, is the miracle of the quilting process. To make a quilt, we plan, sketch, draft, choose color and fabric, cut, pin, sew, press,

assemble, miter, baste, quilt, bind, and label. All these elements, in concert with one another, make up the process I will speak of throughout this book. Each element is important to the success of the whole. Care throughout the process ensures a successful quilt. Garments, bed quilts, wall hangings, miniatures, and small scale quilts all follow this process. Love for fabric, color, and creativity binds all quilters to the process.

As I share with you my approach to successful small scale quiltmaking, my love of the process will be the focus of this book. Wherever your own quilting path leads you, I encourage you to remain true to yourself. Make quilts that please you. Listen for guidance from your own heart. Your most beautiful work is there, patiently waiting for you to call.

Piece,

Sally

HOW, WHAT, AND WHY

HOW TO USE THIS BOOK

To get the most from this book, read it through before beginning any of the projects. An overview of the process relative to small scale quiltmaking will make the specifics of the projects easier to execute. Included are many hints, suggestions, and ideas to help you develop precision sewing skills, increase your knowledge of color and fabric choices, and encourage your creativity. The information I have included is what has given me the most satisfying results in the most efficient manner. As is every quiltmaker I know, I am always open to learning new ways to improve the process, expand my growth, and continually improve the quality of my work. The process I follow, and teach, mirrors large scale quiltmaking, with some subtle but important differences.

The projects are presented in order of their degree of skill. There are creative challenges for both new and experienced quilters. I have explained the techniques or methods that best answer the challenges of each project. With maximum accuracy and efficient execution as my guiding standards, there are complete, detailed instructions for cutting and sewing. You simply have to bring a little willingness to try, and a large expectation to have fun. Successful small scale quiltmaking is no more difficult than large scale quiltmaking. It does, however, require a bit more time, patience, and desire to accomplish. Working at a smaller scale is a challenging and rewarding process. My hope is that you find small scale quiltmaking an exciting addition to your world of quiltmaking and that this book will be helpful to all who are striving for their personal best.

WHAT IS SMALL SCALE QUILTMAKING?

I describe what I do as "small scale" rather than "miniature" for two reasons. One is that I do not work in a specific one-inch to one-foot scale. The other is that my creative perspective "sees" full size. I then transfer that view to a smaller scale of my own choosing. My main goal is to produce a beautiful quilt. The fun part of challenging my creative and technical skills is enjoying the process of producing a beautiful quilt. The size of the finished quilt is not a key consideration. I reduce the work to a scale that is comfortable yet challenging, and is faithful to the balance and symmetry of my original vision. I create quilts to excite my eye, challenge my hand, and faithfully reflect my "full-size" vision, in a smaller space.

My perspective is always full size, not miniature. My thoughts, dreams, designs, images, and plans are all full size. Only my sewing is small. I put the same close attention to detail and design expected in a full scale quilt into my small scale work. "Seeing" in full size helps to maintain those opportunities for detail

that define a beautiful quilt. Pieced, mitered, and multiple borders, varied prints and scales for visual texture, broad color spectrums, complex piecing, good proportion, balance, and accurate and precise sewing are the important details that add integrity to any successful quilt, whatever the size. It is the process of quiltmaking that I love.

The piecing I do is not fast or production-line oriented. It is a deliberate, orchestrated, slow, relaxed approach that maximizes the enjoyment of each step in the process. I enjoy the doing, feeling the cloth, and being in the process, as much as completing the project.

WHY MAKE SMALL SCALE QUILTS?

Working small involves a definite time-saving element. Please understand, however, that the time saving comes when it is time to quilt. Since the final quilt is often smaller, it will require fewer quilting stitches. However, because of the smaller size of the quilt, I often include a larger quantity of elaborate and intricate quilting. Remember, I am in it for the pleasure of the process, not the speed of the project. Each of us must find our own purpose and pleasure in what we do, and there are no right or wrong issues in the pursuit of those individual goals.

The size of any work determines tolerance for errors. In small scale quiltmaking, the tolerance is quite close. Each discrepancy is magnified, and the visual effect is instantly obvious. Working within these small margins improves the skills of even the best sewer. Our skills rise to meet the challenges we are willing to confront. To be successful, small scale quilts ask us for a little more time and patience. They give us a higher skill level, a better understanding of the process, and a lifetime of continuous improvement and growth.

Small scale quilts beautifully enhance garments. A jacket of mine that contains many small pieced blocks drew a very interesting comment from a *Threads* magazine staff member. To paraphrase, she observed that she often sees jackets and vests "wear" people, but she could clearly see that I was wearing my jacket. This comment clarifies the meaning and importance of scale and proportion. Thinking large and working small has helped me to develop a better understanding of the scale and proportion decisions that must be carefully considered for any size project.

Small scale piecework provides us the opportunity to stretch and grow. I am much more likely to experiment with color or design if I know the commitment is only weeks or days rather than months. The process of creating in a smaller scale is faster, and more ideas can emerge, develop, and evolve over the same time we might spend on one full size project. The more we use our creativity, the more creative we become. The more creative we become, the more clearly we see with our spiritual vision, and the more connected, or whole, we are.

Small scale piecework is very effective in larger quilts. Varying the sizes of the same block, and/or placing a smaller block inside a larger one, can achieve dramatic effects with repeat block quilts. My *Stepping Out* quilt displays both ideas.

Small quilts offer opportunities to give from the heart more often. They do not require the eight to twelve months of hand quilting that a full scale quilt might demand. The more we give, the more we receive in return, and size has nothing to do with a gift from the heart.

Using small scale quilts to decorate your home much as you would artwork adds feelings of warmth and comfort. Quilts seem to say welcome to all who enter, and invite everyone to relax and linger a little longer.

These are a few reasons why working in this scale is fun and exciting. Translating a full sized idea into a small scale wall hanging, or a framed piece, is an exciting challenge that requires a well-executed process. As quiltmakers we share a passion for fabric, color, design, sewing, and quilting. We make quilts for friends, family, home decorating, display, competition, and sometimes simply for the delight and love of the doing. None of this has anything to do with size. The process for full scale and small scale quiltmaking is the same; only the size of the result is different. The challenge of working small while maintaining the detail and integrity of full scale is an exhilarating process.

You will be missing a great deal if you do not explore the joy and satisfaction that come from small scale quiltmaking. Small scale quilts have warmed my heart and touched my soul. Those same miracles are yours for a little willingness to try.

INGREDIENTS
FOR
SUCCESS

Friends and students have asked me what I do to create successful blocks consistently and with little difficulty. I have tried to evaluate and examine what I do specifically so that I might share that with you. Time, experience (practice), and a love of quiltmaking are all you need to accomplish successful small scale quilts. I do not have any special tricks or talents; I simply execute each individual element of the process the best I can and in a logical sequence. My joy comes from the journey. The following elements, in concert with one another, contribute toward successful small scale quilts.

1. Be willing to make mistakes and then correct them. For some reason we seem to equate making a mistake with being a failure. Mistakes are positive tools to help us learn, grow, and improve. The common task of removing stitches and resewing is a necessary process which improves our skills. If something is technically or creatively in question, or if in your heart you know something is not just right, acknowledge it. Change or correct it quickly. (A mistake is a function of how serious it is, and how long we allow it to last.) At this small scale, the smallest mistakes are magnified. Finding satisfaction by doing your best is more important and valuable than the small amount of time it takes to remove a few stitches and resew. Reaching for your best feels good!

   Quiltmaking is a continuous process. If we do not make mistakes, we are not pushing ourselves beyond our comfort zones. Growth comes when we leave our comfort zones. The real issue about mistakes is not that we make them, but how we react to them.

2. Time is the essential ingredient of successful small scale quiltmaking. It takes time to be accurate—to pin precisely, to sew slowly, to press carefully; but this is forward time. By that I mean if you try to rush or take shortcuts, you will have to remove stitches and resew unnecessarily. That will require the same amount of time you would use if you were pinning and sewing slowly, but continually moving forward. There will always be times when removing stitches and resewing is necessary. I just do not want to waste time removing stitches because I did not want to put in a pin. It's okay to move slowly, particularly if you are moving forward.

3. Visualize the project in full scale. To successfully create small scale quilts you must "see" the quilt in full size. This allows you the opportunity to include in the small design all the detail and integrity of full size elements.

Variety of color and fabric, sophisticated and interesting sets, detailed or pieced borders, good proportion, and quilting detail are as important at small scale as they are at full size. As you approach each project, begin by visualizing it as a full size quilt.

4. Develop good sewing skills. Accuracy when cutting, marking, and sewing ensures good sewing skills and successful work. Maintaining that accuracy requires practice, experience, and time to develop and improve. Doing my personal best, learning and improving, then passing it on through teaching, is most important to me. Perfection is not my goal, continuous improvement is.

How well we execute the process contributes toward the total success of the work. You will only improve through experience, mistakes, and successes. I make lots of mistakes. I try to correct them as best I can, learn from them, and continue. It's the journey that I love, remember?

TOOLS AND EQUIPMENT

Besides the usual quiltmaking tools, I also use the following to help create successful small scale quilts.

- **Mirrors**—two ($3\frac{1}{2}$" x 6" approx.) mirrors taped together at one end to "see" how corners turn or how multiples of fabric will appear.

- **Instant Camera**—Quickly photograph work in progress, change it around to get different looks, evaluate it, and be able to move the blocks back to their original position without having to sketch or remember.

- **Multifaceted Viewer**—an inexpensive tool (found in toy shops) to see multiples of one block, to place those blocks on square or on point, and to see how the color is working.

- **Stiletto**—a pointed tool used as an extension of your hand.

- **Small Rotary Cutter**—easy to hold and control.

- **$\frac{1}{16}$" Hole Punch**—an invaluable tool for template making.

- **Pins** —I use very long, fine pins with glass heads ($1\frac{3}{8}$" long and .50mm diameter).

- **Rulers**—I use a 3" x 18" Omnigrid® ruler with a continuous $\frac{1}{8}$" grid marked with very fine black lines both horizontally and vertically. I also use a 4" square Omnigrid ruler with the above-mentioned black line $\frac{1}{8}$" grid and the 6" Bias Square®. (Use your preferred brand of rulers.)

- **Reducing Glass**—gives distance from the work, and allows evaluation of fabric, color, and value choices.

- **Quilter's Glu Tube®**—allows me to create very small appliqué shapes successfully and easily. Do not confuse this with a glue stick.

- **Hot Tape™**—holds appliqué shapes in place instead of thread basting. You can iron on it, remove it with no residue, and reuse it.

- **Metal Bias or Celtic Bars™**—I prefer metal to other materials because metal forms a flat, well-creased bias piece.

- **Zippered Baggies**—handy for storing templates, completed blocks, or blocks in progress so they can be seen and shared without handling.

- **Sandpaper Board**—can be made from a 12" or 13" square of masonite with a sheet of very fine sandpaper glued to it.

- **Tweezers**—helpful in removing small paper shapes from appliqué work.

- **Straight Stitch Throat Plate**—optional but very helpful.

- **Sewing Machine Needle**—I use a Schmetz Universal 80/12.

- **Sewing Thread**—I use 100 percent cotton Mettler Machine Embroidery Thread 60/2 in a medium tan or gray color that seems to blend well with most fabrics. This is a finer thread and therefore takes up less space and creates flatter seams.

- **Round Wooden Toothpick**—I find this an invaluable tool to scoot fabric under when appliquéing. The wooden toothpick gently grasps the cotton fabric and makes it very easy to manipulate. It is also helpful if a knot reappears and you need to push it back into the quilt.

- **Flannel Board**—30" x 40" foam-core board, covered with flannel, to use for designing. You can pin into it and take it to your machine. This is a middle step between a sandpaper board and a flannel wall.

COLOR AND FABRIC

Quilts project personality and express emotion through the colors and fabrics we choose. Color is what gives quilts visual impact. Although several people might make the same design, the colors and fabrics they choose make each quilt a unique reflection of the maker. We respond to color more than to any other element of the quilt. As in full scale quiltmaking, the challenge is to create a beautiful quilt that is balanced in color and design, will embrace viewers from a distance, and which draws them into the quilt.

COLOR

Most of what I do with color and fabric feels intuitive. Nevertheless, I do follow a routine and apply specific guidelines to arrive at that intuitive feeling.

Include several shades of the chosen colors. An intense or bright value of one color will add interesting sparkle. This color is often strong, and should be used in small amounts. Be careful not to prejudge what works and what does not. Interview the fabrics and colors by cutting small pieces (by eye) to see how they interact with other fabrics you have already chosen. A bright orange three-inch square might be quite overwhelming, while a half-inch piece of the same fabric might add the perfect bit of sparkle. The smaller the piece, the more intense you can be with color.

Finding a fabric or color that "matches" perfectly seems logical, but is not always wise. If you have a green in your palette fabric, add another shade of green to your quilt. This creates more interest, and increases variety.

Also, include one very dark color in your fabric choices. This will serve to separate, outline, and define areas, and give the eye a resting place. Often this very dark color will give the quilt order and unity by serving as an anchor.

You can approach your color choices from various directions. I offer the following suggestions as a springboard for your own creativity.

1. Think about how you want the quilt to look and feel. For example, an "old fashioned" look conjures up colors that are warm, such as tan, beige, brown, rust, orange, gold, and red. The visual texture of the chosen fabrics should support the theme. The same "old fashioned" look could mean plaids, calicoes, and small florals. Perhaps you want a soft, pastel baby quilt, or a patriotic theme, a romantic feel, a dramatic look, an Amish style quilt, or a contemporary style. These themes can be expressed through the thoughtful selection of color and fabrics. A 1930s look or feel was my goal for the *Pieced Double Wedding Ring* quilt included in The Projects, page 78.

Palette Fabric

2. Choose a multicolored fabric that you like, and from that "palette" fabric choose several coordinating colors, varying their value and visual texture. Using a "palette" fabric is a way to build confidence. You might not use the palette fabric itself in the quilt, but may use only the colors in the fabric!

3. You might choose to work in just two colors, for example, red and purple. Choose several different reds from pink to very dark red, and purples from lavender to blue-violet. Vary the visual texture of the fabrics. Expand and stretch the color.

4. You might decide to make a seasonal quilt, which would guide your color choices. For example, Christmas would traditionally mean reds, greens, and gold . Thanksgiving would be expressed in golds, reds, and yellows of the changing season. Easter, of course, would encompass the purples, lavenders, yellows, pinks, and greens of spring.

5. The beauty of nature has inspired many quilts and quiltmakers. Quiltmakers incorporate the colors of sunsets, seascapes, deserts, mountains, sunrises, etc., into all sizes and types of projects.

6. Looking at pictures of quilts in books and magazines is also a good way to find a color scheme or look that inspires you.

When you have selected the colors, be sure to include different values of those colors, including an intense or bright, and a very dark color. These three elements in combination with each other play a significant role in making a successful small scale quilt.

Choosing color and fabric can be stressful. I continue to struggle with these decisions, but am learning to listen to my heart and trust my instinct and intuition. A willingness to make mistakes helps me through this decision process. We gain experience from doing. It's as important to know what doesn't work as it is to know what does. Remember to look for the unexpected benefit in your errors. It's always there.

Shading

VALUE

Value is the lightness or darkness of a color. It is also relative and relies on the surrounding values to define itself. For example, a medium value fabric may appear light when surrounded by a dark value fabric and dark if surrounded by a light value fabric.

Small scale quilts benefit from using many different values of one color to create movement and smoothness. Before you can choose colors and fabrics you must evaluate the design and decide what areas will be light, medium, and dark. Value placement creates design. Once you have chosen the fabrics you want to use, separating them into piles of light, medium, and dark makes it easier to make choices.

CONTRAST

Contrast is the difference between values. You can have high contrast between fabrics, or subtle, low contrast. Contrast defines design. The higher the contrast, the clearer the image. The lower the contrast, the more subtle the image becomes. Small scale quiltmaking benefits from high, exaggerated contrast between the background area and the design elements. You should be able to "read" the quilt from a distance to appreciate the work.

VISUAL TEXTURE

Visual texture is the size and style of the print on the fabric. Successful quilts, large and small, require special attention to the visual texture of the fabrics chosen. Combining fabrics of plaid, check, paisley, floral, geometric, and stripe designs, with tone-on-tone, or low activity prints and border prints, all contribute to the success of the quilt.

Visual Texture

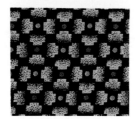

Busy Fabrics

Tone-on-tone fabrics often read as solids, but give a subtle texture. They are usually one color in two shades with a print. They offer low activity, quietness, and smoothness without distraction as well as support for larger, more active prints. They also clarify and define design.

Border prints dress up quilts and add an elegant, sophisticated feeling. Remember, we are creating a full size image in a small scale. We want to include detail, and printed fabric is one way to do that. Note the border prints in *Mosaic Mask*, page 58; *Stepping Out*, page 83; and *Ohio Sampler*, page 70. Vary the visual textures of the fabrics to add interest and keep the eye moving. If you were to use all small prints, the quilt would be flat and visually uninteresting.

I like to include as many different fabrics and shades of color in my quilts as I can. Most of the time I am happy with the results. I usually avoid fabrics with a lot of white space in them or those that are too busy. Fabrics with sharp contrast between the background and the other colors can be distracting.

Recognize that some fabrics play a lead role in the quilt and others play supporting roles. Make choices and decisions that are necessary to begin, but be flexible and willing to change as you work through the process of creating the quilt. If I cut a fabric that just does not work, I interview others until I find the one that is best for my quilt. Do not settle!

FABRIC SELECTION AND PREPARATION

I suggest using good quality, 100 percent cotton fabric. My personal preference is to pre-wash and dry my fabrics before using them.

When fabric shopping, I look for interesting prints and colors, not just fabrics I love. Try to imagine how prints would look cut small. Take along a 3" x 5" card with small shapes (squares, triangles, etc.) cut out that you can place on bolts of fabric to "see" how they look cut small. I also am interested in multicolored fabrics with no white in them. If the colors are wonderful but the print is not, I buy it anyway and use it as a palette fabric (page 18).

I prefer working with quarter-yard pieces of fabric (9" x 42") because it gives me the most versatility. That size will yield 12"–13" of manageable bias length. The cross grain length for borders (40"–42") works well, and the 9" of lengthwise grain is comfortable when cutting and sewing strips together. I do not worry much about running out of a particular fabric because I find it challenging and fun to have to find another fabric that works. If I find a fabric I cannot live without, I buy three yards.

CONSTRUCTION TECHNIQUES

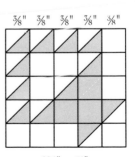

S ome of these techniques are new, some exist already. All contribute toward successful small scale quiltmaking if done with care and accuracy. I have included suggestions that may be helpful when working in a smaller scale.

GRID DIMENSION

We draft most patchwork blocks on grids of equal divisions down and across.

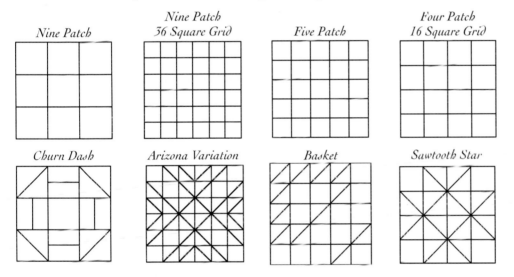

Nine Patch

Nine Patch 36 Square Grid

Five Patch

Four Patch 16 Square Grid

Churn Dash

Arizona Variation

Basket

Sawtooth Star

The grid dimension determines the size of the block. You could approach this in two ways.

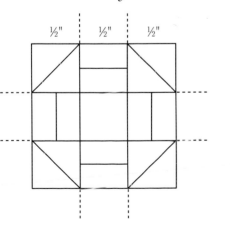

½" ½" ½"

1. Decide the block size first and then divide that by the number of divisions across. For example, a Churn Dash block has three equal divisions across and down. If you wanted a $1\frac{1}{2}$" block, you would divide $1\frac{1}{2}$" by three, and that would give you a grid dimension of $\frac{1}{2}$".

2. I often choose the grid dimension first and then multiply that by the number of divisions across to get the block size. When working in a repeat block format, the size of the block is not as important as working in a grid dimension that is comfortable. For example, the small basket block in *Shadow Baskets*, page 92, is based on five equal divisions across and down. I know from my experience that a $\frac{3}{8}$" grid dimension is comfortable for me. If I multiply $\frac{3}{8}$" x 5 = $\frac{15}{8}$" or $1\frac{7}{8}$", which would be the block size finished (with no seam allowance).

$\frac{3}{8}$" $\frac{3}{8}$" $\frac{3}{8}$" $\frac{3}{8}$" $\frac{3}{8}$"

$\frac{15}{8}$" = $1\frac{7}{8}$"

³⁄₈" Grid

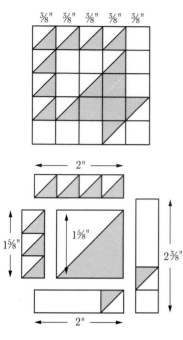

Knowing the grid dimension also enables me to measure as I sew and make any corrections or adjustments easily. It's not fun to get a whole block sewn and discover it does not measure what it should, or to get units of a block sewn and discover they do not join smoothly. Any discrepancy in small scale quilts is magnified. Staying attentive to accuracy is important.

The grid dimension does not include seam allowances. To be able to measure your work as you sew, just add up the number of grids you have sewn together, multiply that by the established grid dimension you've chosen, then add ¹⁄₂" for seam allowance. When a unit takes up multiple grids, determine how many and multiply that number by the established grid dimension. Then add ¹⁄₂" for seam allowance.

I find this method of maintaining accuracy invaluable. Measuring after sewing also enables you to quickly identify any discrepancy that occurs from the last seam sewn. Yes, this takes a little time, but it is time well spent. Grid dimensions are given for the projects in this book where appropriate and relevant.

CUTTING ACCURATELY

Accuracy is the heart of successful small scale quiltmaking. Accuracy when you cut fabric, either with scissors or the rotary cutter, ensures a good beginning. If you are off just ¹⁄₁₆" over four seams, you have accumulated a ¹⁄₄" discrepancy, and if the block size is only 1¹⁄₂", that ¹⁄₄" discrepancy can be disastrous.

Rotary Cutting

In my teaching experience I have found that when quilters rotary cut they often misplace the ruler on their fabric. Imagine you are cutting a one-inch strip off your yardage. After developing a straight angle, many quilters position the ruler so that the one-inch line is butted against or just next to the cut edge of their fabric. When you do this, you lose the dimension of the line. You must lift the ruler and place the one-inch line on the edge of the fabric…an accurate one-inch cut includes the one-inch line on the ruler. In small scale quiltmaking thread takes up a significant amount of space, so including the line when you cut specific dimensions gives the thread a place to be.

I prefer using the small rotary cutter with the three rulers described in Tools and Equipment, page 15. The fine black lines on the rulers are important to me because although I do not sew with a ¹⁄₈" seam allowance, I often cut in ¹⁄₈" increments. These rulers are easy and clear to read.

Refer to your favorite basic quiltmaking or rotary cutting book for instructions on developing a straight edge on the fabric and cutting squares and rectangles from strips.

Triangles

Triangles for the projects in this book are cut in several different ways, depending on their size, grain placement, and how many are needed of a particular fabric. Each project specifies which method I feel is the most successful in each individual case.

Half-Square Triangle Units—Bias Strip Method

Two right-angle triangles join to create a square. Creating this type of unit from bias strips is an accurate method that adapts beautifully to small scale quiltmaking. I first became aware of this technique from books by Marsha McCloskey. Although I cut my half square triangle units from the bias strip unit a little differently, the idea is the same. To create two half-square triangles that are already joined and trimmed, do the following (specific widths and lengths of strips will be given with the appropriate projects):

1. Pair two desired fabrics, right sides together, and press.

2. Develop a true bias cut as illustrated, then cut the desired width of strips.

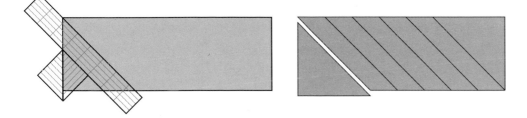

3. Sew the two strips down the length with a $1/4$" seam allowance. Press seam open and trim. Refer to page 29–31 for Pressing and Trimming instructions.

4. To cut the desired size half-square triangle units from the bias strips you need to first establish a 45° angle on the strip unit. Place the 45° line of the square ruler on the seam, not on the edge of the fabric. The ruler is now the appropriate angle for cutting. Next, position the long ruler next to the square ruler firmly, move the square ruler away, and cut along the long ruler edge.

5. Using the long ruler, cut the desired width of slices from the two-strip unit, always keeping the 45° line of the ruler on the seam and the chosen dimension line of the ruler on the edge. Aligning both lines as described ensures an accurately angled cut. When you cannot position the two lines as described, that suggests the angle is off and you need to reestablish the angle as described in Step 4 and proceed again. Keeping the 45° line on the seam when cutting appropriate width slices contributes toward equally split squares.

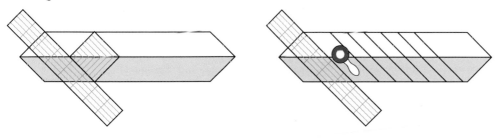

6. From the slices, cut squares as illustrated, continuing to keep the 45° line on the seam.

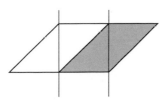

Oversized Half-Square Triangle Units

Another technique that is successful, accurate, and makes it easy to use a variety of fabrics.

1. Cut two squares larger than you need of two appropriate fabrics.

2. Draw a diagonal line on the wrong side of the lightest one. Pair it to the other square, right sides together, and sew on the line.

3. Trim to within $1/4$" of stitches, open seam with hands, then iron and trim seam allowance again to a generous $1/8$".

4. Using the Bias Square®, fine cut the oversized half-square triangle unit to the desired size, using the seam as a guide.

I use this method when I want a few units from many fabrics. It is also a very successful method for quilters who are new to this scale of work.

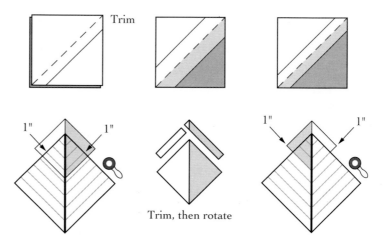

Double Half-Square Triangle Units

I first saw this technique in the book *Quilts, Quilts, Quilts* by Diana McClun and Laura Nownes. The technique is used here to make star points, but could also be Flying Geese or other similar units. The unit consists of three triangles. To sew the unit you will use a rectangle and two squares.

Projects that use this technique are the *Ohio Sampler*, page 70, and *Stepping Out*, page 83. Each project will give specific cutting and sewing directions. Create the unit as follows:

1. Cut a rectangle and two squares of chosen fabric.

2. Draw a diagonal line on the wrong side of each square.

3. Place one square onto the rectangle at one end, right sides together, and sew just on the scrap side of the line (the scrap side is the side that gets trimmed). Thread takes up space, so sewing on the scrap side of the line gives the space back.

4. Flip the square's corner to meet the rectangle's corner. If the corners meet to your standards, trim away the square's corner only, to within $1/8$" of the stitches, leaving the rectangle in place.
   Note: I leave the rectangle in place as a safety net feature in the event the corners do not quite meet. If that happens, when you join this unit to something else you would use the edge of the rectangle as your guide, not the edge of the square.

5. After trimming the corner, press to the square. Add the second square at the other end of the rectangle, taking care to position the second diagonal line correctly, and sewing just on the scrap side of the drawn line. Trim and press as described earlier.

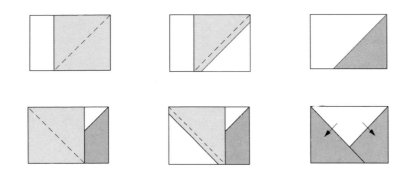

TEMPLATES

Templates are guides used for cutting angular or curved shapes from fabric. Accurate templates, which include $1/4$" seam allowance, ensure accurate work. When templates are needed I like to mark the sewing line on the templates and punch a hole at each intersection, which allows me to insert a pen or pencil into the hole and make a dot on the fabric. These dots are used as guides when pinning one shape onto another so that the pieces are aligned properly for sewing. When making templates I use a permanent black pen to mark dots at intersections and a No. 2 pencil to mark all other information. This gives me the flexibility to change or correct by erasing.

1. Place a manageable-size piece of template plastic material over the shape needed. Dot each intersection and almost connect the dots, leaving them obvious and apparent for piercing or punching.

2. Mark an accurate $1/4$" seam allowance on all sides of each shape. Also mark where to cut off tips, if appropriate.

3. Write the name and size of the block, identifying letter, and grain line on each template.

4. Cut out each template accurately, cutting the drawn line off.

5. Punch holes at the dots with a $1/16$" hole punch; or place the template face down on a thick towel and carefully pierce the plastic with a stiletto, large needle, or similar tool and twist gently, taking care not to crack the plastic. The hole should be large enough to insert a pencil or pen to mark a dot on the fabric. The $1/8$" hole punch creates too large a hole and makes it difficult to dot the fabric accurately.

Before cutting into your fabric, place the templates onto one another as if you were sewing. Because the template shapes interrelate to each other, the edges and holes should line up.

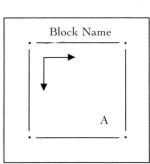

Marking Fabric with Templates

When using templates to mark fabric, place each template face down on the wrong side of the fabric. Reverse templates will be placed right side up. Trace around the template, angling the marking tool into the edge of the template (this is the cutting line). Dot each intersection hole (if these dots were connected, you would create your sewing line). Cut out each shape accurately, cutting the line off.

To prevent the fabric from shifting, place the fabric on a sandpaper board and hold the template shape firmly while tracing.

SEWING ACCURATELY

Accurate sewing is the soul of successful small scale quiltmaking. If you have cut accurately and now sew accurately, your work will go together smoothly, much like a puzzle.

$^1/_4$" Seam Allowance

Assuming you have cut with an accurate $^1/_4$" seam allowance, you must now sew with the same seam allowance to ensure a successful, accurate block or quilt. One way to check your $^1/_4$" accuracy is to cut two 1" x $3^1/_2$" strips of any fabric, pair them and sew down the length with an accurate $^1/_4$" seam allowance and a large stitch length (in case you need to remove the stitches and retest). Open the two-strip unit and press. This unit should now measure $1^1/_2$" from edge to edge. If it does, you are cutting and sewing accurately. If it does not, your cutting or sewing is in question and you need to make an appropriate adjustment.

A rumor is going around in the quilt community that says if you are just a little off it does not really matter as long as you stay consistently off and use the same machine. Sound familiar? It does to me, too. Experience, however, has taught me to question this standard of quality. If you are sewing a 3" block that has 45 pieces and numerous seams to a 3" block that has only 5 pieces and minimal seams, you must sew with an accurate $^1/_4$" seam allowance or the two blocks will be different sizes and will not sew together very smoothly. The smaller the block, the more crucial accuracy becomes.

Sewing Straight

I find this to be a most overlooked area of accurate, precise sewing. To sew straight, that is, to enter onto the fabric at $^1/_4$", stay at $^1/_4$", and exit off the fabric at $^1/_4$", is crucial to successful small scale quiltmaking. As you begin to sew, be sure the pieces of fabric are positioned or registered onto one another correctly and "squarely". Sit directly in front of your needle so that you see the sewing path clearly.

You will often be sewing short distances, so how you enter and exit the fabric will impact on the accuracy and squareness of the piece. Unknowingly, many of us enter onto the fabric casually, perhaps a little deep of $^1/_4$". Then we straighten out to $^1/_4$", and when we get near the end we let go so we can pick up the next pieces while the previous piece sews itself off, often at less than $^1/_4$". This results in what I describe as wavy sewing, which can create problems in small scale work.

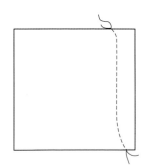

Sewing Slowly

Sew slowly—think of yourself as hand sewing with an electric needle and be sure the sewing machine needle enters and exits the fabric exactly where you want. I hold my work firmly with my left hand as I guide it under the needle and often use the stiletto to help keep the raw edges of the fabric against whatever seam guide I am using. Most machines will pull your fabric to the left as you get to the end of the sewing line. Using the stiletto to hold the edges in place helps to exit the fabric at $1/4$".

Uneven Edges

When appropriate, be sure edges are even and matched. If one edge drops below the other while sewing, you have not taken equal seam allowances on both pieces, which can make your work measure inaccurately even when you are sewing with an accurate $1/4$" seam allowance.

Measuring and Maintaining the Grid Dimension

This one element will enable you to monitor your work and identify what seam needs adjusting, if any. Refer to page 21 for specifics on Grid Dimension.

Stitch Length

After testing for an accurate $1/4$" seam allowance, I adjust the stitch length to approximately 12–15 stitches per inch. You want to be sure the stitch length is not too small and draws up or gathers the fabric, or is too small to remove easily. I often change the length of the sewing stitch depending on what I am doing. If I am experimenting, or if I am unsure about matching a heavily seamed center, I increase the stitch length so that if I need to remove the stitches I can easily do so and resew. If my sewing meets my standards, I resew over the thread with a smaller stitch. Adjusting the stitch length when doing Y-seaming or inset seaming (page 102) is helpful as well; it allows you to sew very close to the $1/4$" reference dot without actually sewing into it.

Sewing Thread Type and Color

I use Mettler 100 percent Cotton Machine Embroidery thread 60/2 in the top and bobbin of my sewing machine. This thread is fine and strong and takes up less space, which results in flatter seams. I encourage you to try this thread when doing small work. You will be amazed at the difference.

I generally use a medium or muddy tan or gray color thread, which blends into most of the fabrics. Matching color is not as important as blending or camouflaging. You do not want to see thread from the right side of the work. My rule of thumb is to choose a dark thread color in relation to the fabric. If I were working in black and white, I would probably use black thread. Some blocks create more opportunity for thread to show, as in a LeMoyne Star where eight seams meet in the center. Open seams are another opportunity for thread to show. Be attentive to the thread color.

Feeding Fabric Under the Needle Smoothly

1. Sew on a scrap piece of fabric first, then feed "real" pieces behind it. When all the "real" pieces are through the needle, cut off the scrap, bring it around to the front, and sew on it, cutting off the "real" pieces. As a result, you are

not pulling the work out from the machine and clipping threads. You sew tidier with less thread. The machine takes on small pieces easier if it is already sewing, and you will not continually lift the presser foot up and down.

2. Use the stiletto as an extension of your hand to help guide your work under the needle straight and to keep the edges against whatever seam guide you use. This tool helps you to manipulate small pieces. A wooden skewer, toothpick, seam ripper, or large pin would also work.

3. A straight stitch throat plate (the one with the tiny round hole) lessens the opportunity for the machine to "eat" small pieces. Leave needle in center position, for obvious reasons.

4. Change the sewing machine needle after fifteen to twenty hours of use.

5. If you find the machine seems to shift the two pieces of fabric being sewn by pushing the top layer of fabric first, which creates a small hump as you begin to sew, slightly lift the presser foot to position your work where you want it, then put the foot down. It's more successful to position your work for sewing than to push it under the needle and hope it feeds evenly.

6. If you are doing Y-seam or inset seam construction, or if you do not use a scrap piece of fabric ahead of your work, you will need to hold the threads as you begin sewing. If you do not, you might get a bobbin bulge on the back of your work. If this happens, cut it off and begin again.

7. Placing a thin piece of paper underneath the fabric can help to stabilize it when entering sharp corners.

REMOVING STITCHES

When it becomes necessary to remove stitches and resew, do so carefully, so as not to distress or fray the fabric. Using a seam ripper, cut every third or fourth stitch along the sewing line. Then turn the work over and lift that thread. It will easily release, and the two pieces of fabric can be separated and repositioned for sewing. Careful removal of stitches will allow you to resew the same small pieces of fabric over and over without having to recut.

PINNING

I use long, fine pins ($1^3/_8$" x .50mm) with glass heads. This type of pin slides into fabrics easily and creates little or no distortion on the edge of the fabric when sewing, resulting in a flatter piece for the machine to sew over. I sew over pins successfully without hurting the machine because the combination of slow sewing and fine pins allows the sewing machine needle to either slide in front of or behind the pins. Fast sewing increases the opportunity for the needle to hit a pin and break.

I use pins to secure intersections, match points, ease areas of fullness, keep outside edges even, match dots which help position one piece onto another properly, and sometimes just while transporting work to the machine, then removing them. I use pins whenever it benefits my sewing.

We often pin the same way regardless of the type of seam. Most of us pin perpendicular to the edge, with pin heads to the right as the fabric goes under the needle. This pin positioning can often create humps and bumps and distortion on the edge of the fabric, which can be difficult for your machine to sew over. Positioning the pin heads to the left creates a much flatter path for the machine needle to follow.

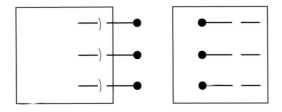

When sewing narrow strips of fabric together, pinning parallel to the edge and drawing the pins out as you approach them creates less distortion than pinning perpendicular to the edge.

Matching points and intersections successfully requires careful pinning, accurate straight sewing, well-planned pressing, and time, but is easily accomplished. After sewing, if the point or intersection is not matched, only two possible things could have happened: your pinning and/or sewing needs improvement. It's very easy to remove a few stitches, repin, and resew. It's not as if you only get one try. I remove stitches and resew as many times as it takes to accomplish the task successfully.

To match some seams I use what is referred to as a **positioning pin**. This pin precisely **matches** one point to another; it does **not secure** the area. It keeps the two pieces together while registering, or positioning, them onto one another and creating even edges. An additional pin, usually positioned just to the left of the seam, secures the area and the positioning pin is removed.

PRESSING

Pressing is setting a seam with heat and pressure, with a dry iron or with steam, by lifting the iron and setting it down. Sliding the iron around is ironing. Pressing, not ironing, is very important and contributes greatly to the success of this work. I press seams to one side or sometimes open; occasionally I collapse seams. Ideally, you want to create opposing seams for easy matching of points. When that is not possible, press to create as flat a piece as possible and distribute the bulk.

Pressing each seam helps to get the maximum measurement. Arrange and manipulate the fabric with your hands before touching it with the iron. Pressing can either distort your work or help you reshape it. The direction you press the seam allowances when you begin pinning units and rows together can sometimes make a large difference in how smoothly the sewing goes. Pressing the seams in one direction could round out a point. Pressing them in the opposite direction could sharpen the point, and opening the seam could improve it even more and distribute the bulk. Poor pressing can distort beautiful piecing.

When I begin I use a hot dry iron, and as my work grows and accumulates bulk I use steam. Be careful the steam does not distort the edges of your fabric. Running your fingernail along the stitches of a newly sewn seam (finger-pressing) and/or pressing the stitches before final pressing relaxes the thread and will nestle the stitches into the fabric.

Open a seam by first combing your nail down the seam. When you do this, you will feel the two fabrics separate and the threads relax. A good open seam requires the two fabrics to be separated down to the thread. After opening the seam with your hands, use your iron carefully to press both from the back and the front. Now trim the seam allowances to a generous $1/8"$ by scissor cutting up one side and then the other. Often I'm asked why not rotary cut the seam allowance before opening, and my response is that it is much easier to trim an open seam than to open a trimmed seam. Yes, it takes a little more time, but it is well worth it.

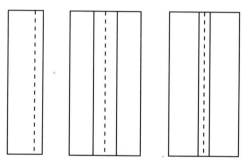

Note: The projects will identify pressing paths by using arrows to indicate direction and an "o" to indicate an open seam.

Collapsing seams helps to distribute and reduce bulk and can be done on a simple, straight, four-seam intersection. To collapse a seam, simply remove, (do not cut), the vertical stitches in the seam allowance at the intersection, one at a time, to the last horizontal line of stitching on both pieces. With your hands, arrange the seam allowances in opposite directions and then press.

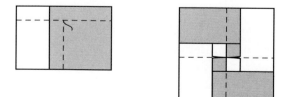

When the quilt top or block is complete, do a final steam pressing, carefully manipulating, if necessary, the fabric into shape. One way to block your work is to draw the desired size on a piece of muslin, lightly dampen the block, and pin into place. Then gently either stretch the edges to meet the guidelines, or pat inward to meet them. Steam press and let cool and dry in place before removing pins. Cotton is very forgiving and allows minor adjustments easily. Final pressing from the top on a soft towel allows the seams to sink into the towel and makes the top look flatter.

TRIMMING SEAMS

The projects in this book use a $1/4$" seam allowance. If you have a 3" block, for example, that has 40 or 50 pieces in it, and all those pieces have a $1/4$" seam allowance on all their sides, you can imagine the bulk that will accumulate. To help distribute and release bulk, trim seams to a generous $1/8$". I trim whether the seam is open or not. Creating a well-sewn, flat, accurate block in a small scale requires trimmed seam allowances.

1. Do not trim too much or the seam allowance will stand straight up rather than press to one side or the other. This condition can create more quilting problems than anything else.

2. You must also know your work is correct before trimming the seam allowance. If you trim your seams and then discover you need to remove stitches and resew, your seam allowance will have been distorted and changed, and resewing could be a little more difficult. This is just one reason why it is so important to maintain grid dimension by monitoring and measuring your work before trimming if possible. If you do trim and then discover you need to remove stitches and resew, you can remove the stitches and measure over from the opposite edge, the grid dimension plus $1/4$", and draw a sewing line.

3. Trim thread close to fabric so work stays neat and tidy.

4. When your block or quilt top is complete, it should have a $1/4$" seam allowance on all sides. Trimming up or squaring up is not a way to correct problems; it should only create straight edges.

BORDERS

A quilt border can have many objectives. Borders contain and frame the quilt, but they also enhance and relate to the quilt's interior with regard to color, fabric, scale, and/or shape. Borders add dimension (size) to the quilt and often establish the dominant color of the quilt. Borders bring the quilt to conclusion. They should make the quilt better than it is without them. Don't settle! The border is part of the whole, not something you quickly add at the end to get finished.

Small scale quilt borders often play a co-starring role with the heart of the quilt. Borders should be proportionate to the quilt's interior to create a pleasing expression. This refers to size relationships among blocks, sashing, or individual shapes within the quilt. Too narrow a border can make a quilt look incomplete and give the feeling you were in a hurry to finish. Too wide a border area can overwhelm the quilt and draw the eye outward rather than inward.

I offer the following suggestions regarding proportion:

1. Choose a total border width first. To help you decide that, evaluate the quilt's interior and use as a starting point the block size or unit size. For example, if I'm using 3" blocks, the border might be approximately 3" wide total. If the blocks are set on point, I measure the diagonal of 3" (4$\frac{1}{4}$") and use that as a starting point.

2. Once I have decided a total width of border (3"), I can determine how I will fragment or break that area up into individual borders of varying widths. The border could include a pieced border and/or multiple strips of fabric. The total width of the multiple borders should be 3".

Trust your eye and your heart. They will not fail you. Be flexible and always keep your quilt's best interest at the forefront. Let it talk, learn to listen.

TYPES OF BORDERS

Multiple Fabric Strips

Borders consisting of multiple, straight strips of fabric are probably the easiest to construct and can be very effective. For example, the *Heritage* project, page 62, uses three different printed fabrics in various widths as its border. The red inner border and the green final border are separated by a black $\frac{1}{8}$" border that adds unexpected detail.

Appliqué Borders

These borders often relate to the quilt in their repetition of a shape from the quilt or a shape that complements a pieced quilt, as the swags do on *Shadow Baskets*, page 92.

Pieced Borders

These borders also relate to the quilt's interior regarding color, fabric, and shape. They are constructed of a repeat unit that relates in size to the interior of the quilt. The *Stepping Out* project, page 83, makes use of a double sawtooth border in two different sizes that relate to the stars.

Combination Borders

This kind of border embraces more than one type, and adds unexpected detail to this scale of work. *Shadow Baskets*, page 92, uses multiple strips of fabric, an appliqué border, and a pieced border.

Border Prints

I've always liked border prints and felt they added elegance and sophistication to quilts. If you evaluate border prints, you will see they consist of varying scales and widths of printed fabric separated from each other by narrow bands, and they all relate in color. I often take note of the narrowest parts of border prints, as they benefit small scale piecing enormously.

I've discovered that you can create your own border prints by choosing two or three different fabrics that have different visual textures (stripes, paisley, florals, plaids, etc.) and relate to the quilt's color and feeling. Cut them at different widths and then separate these fabrics by narrow bands (1/8" or 1/4") of appropriate color that is dark or intense. Remember, the widths of all the strips should add up to the original border width you chose initially.

Work on paper, draft to scale, or simply sketch, but develop a plan or sequence for a border that enhances the quilt. One way to "see" a border is to develop a mock-up of the planned border sequence. Line up your chosen fabrics and fold or lay them on top of each another to see how much will show of each. Then place that group of fabric at the edge of the quilt and place a small mirror at a 45° angle to see how the border will turn. This gives you the opportunity to gather and evaluate lots of information before cutting and sewing. Interview fabrics until you find the best combination for your quilt.

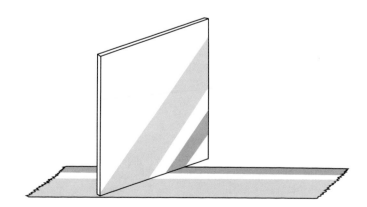

CUTTING BORDERS

Do not cut borders until the interior of the quilt is sewn, so you have the opportunity to interview fabrics and evaluate choices. Cutting border strips from the length grain limits stretching. However, if the fabric size or design prohibits this, I cut on the cross grain. Border prints are usually used lengthwise, so adequate yardage is required. I often cut the final border generously wide, which enables me to "square" up the quilt and prepare it for binding. Always measure the quilt down and across the center to determine border length dimensions.

MITERING CORNERS BY HAND

Take the quilt to the ironing board or a flat surface. Position one corner as illustrated, and using the Bias Square®, check to be sure the corner is "square" and that the fold is in alignment with the 45° angle of the Bias Square. Press, pin, and thread baste in place. Repeat for all four corners. I close the miter permanently by hand appliqué, using well-matched, fine thread and a tiny stitch.

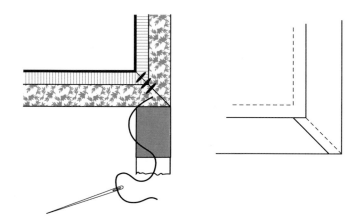

You can leave the miters basted until you are ready to quilt the borders. Then reevaluate the four corners to be sure they have not moved out of alignment during the quilting. If they have, remove the basting, make the necessary adjustments, and hand appliqué closed. Then rebaste the border and continue to quilt or bind. I find this method easy and successful, as it allows me to arrange the miters by hand and create well-turned corners consistently.

Note: When miters are closed by hand appliqué, trim excess to within ¹/₄" of stitches.

BORDER PRINTS WITH MITERED CORNERS

Evaluate the border print and identify motifs or design elements that exist within the border. Then place the center of a motif to the center of the quilt, and place a mirror at the corner of the quilt at a 45° angle to see how the corner will turn. The corners will match and turn if you have the same area of the border print matched to the center of all four sides of a square quilt.

VERY NARROW BORDERS

The technique to create $1/8$" borders consists of two steps. First, oversize the width of the border strips for stability while sewing, and second, trim the appropriate seam allowance to an accurate $1/8$". This cut edge then serves as the sewing guide for adding the next strip. Success in this technique depends on the accurate trimming of the $1/4$" seam allowance to a $1/8$" seam allowance, and very straight sewing along the cut edge of the trimmed seam allowance.

Creating these very narrow borders allows you to use strong and/or intense color proportionately and effectively. The narrow border technique, and complete cutting and sewing instructions to execute it, is included with the instructions for the *Key Chain*, page 48 *Heritage*, page 62; and *Santa Fe*, page 101, quilt projects.

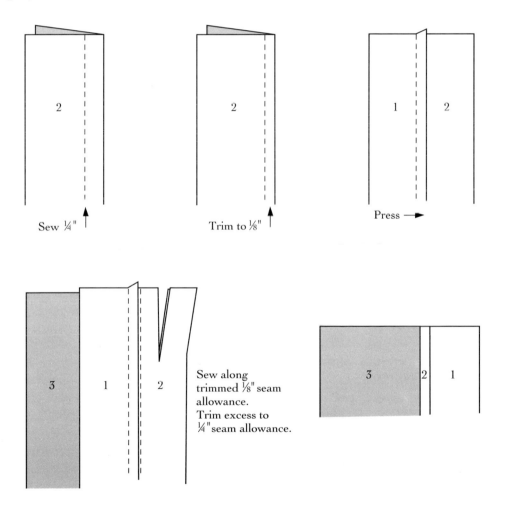

FINISHING TECHNIQUES

Continue to add detail to your quilt as you choose your finishing techniques and styles. Bring your quilt to a lovely conclusion.

BATTING

Batting plays an important role in the finished quilt, as it determines how much loft there will be between the stitches. Knowing what use or purpose the quilt will have is important when you choose batting. Small scale quilts are usually displayed on the wall, framed or free hanging, so visual appearance is primary to function.

I would suggest using a good quality low loft, cotton or cotton/poly blend for hand or machine quilting. It needles well, is flat, and gives an adequate loft. Too flat a batt (flannel, or splitting the batting in half) can make the stitches seem as if they lie on top of the quilt rather than nestling into the fabric.

Cotton and cotton/poly blends, when washed, will shrink up around the stitches and give a flat, old-fashioned, antique appearance to your quilts.

MARKING THE QUILT TOP

I encourage you to do all the marking you can before basting, especially for grids, as they can easily tilt off if you rely on the previous line of stitches. I use a hard lead pencil for light fabrics and a good quality white pencil for dark fabrics. The other tool I use a lot is a chalk wheel, which drops a fine line of chalk when rolled on the fabric next to whatever guide I am using.

Test the marking tools you intend to use on a piece of scrap fabric. Become familiar with how they mark and how they are removed or rubbed off.

If you make a mistake with lead pencil or mark too darkly, you can probably erase a small area with a fabric eraser. If you use an eraser, stabilize the area with your hands and gently rub the fabric. If the area in question is larger, mix three tablespoons of rubbing alcohol and one tablespoon of water with several drops of a mild dishwashing liquid. Using a soft toothbrush, gently rub the penciled area. I use this on light fabrics, and always test on a scrap before using on my quilt.

QUILTING

Quilting is the process of sculpting the quilt. Small scale quilts benefit from adequate, proportioned, well-planned quilting. One of the most pleasurable elements of small scale quilts comes when it's time to put in the stitch. Because these quilts are often significantly smaller than full scale quilts, the time needed to add lots of beautiful stitches is minimal.

Plan all the details of the quilting as if your quilt were full size. My *Santa Fe* quilt, page 101, is heavily quilted. If I were to make that same quilt with 9" blocks instead of 3" blocks, I would still quilt it the same. Think in full scale, do in small scale. Misplaced quilting can distort beautiful piecing, so I often do only seam quilting in the heavily seamed areas, and more elaborate, detailed quilting in side triangles, alternate blocks, and borders. Proportionate designs are necessary to reinforce scale and enhance the quilt, make it better, and give it life.

The quilting design and stitches show more on solid and tone-on-tone fabrics than on fabrics that have much more activity. As you choose fabric, consider the quilting you might do.

Personally, I prefer Gütermann 100 percent cotton quilting thread for its colors, quality, and fineness. A number 12 needle threads easily. Whatever brand thread you choose, work with only about 18" of length at a time.

Contrasting thread color when quilting shows the stitches. Matching thread color shows the relief the quilting stitches create. Give this some thought. I often change color of quilting thread depending on what I want to see. In the *Heritage* project, page 62, the feather wreath is quilted with a burgundy thread, contrasting with the background. I did that to clarify and define the design. All other quilting is done with a thread color that matches the background.

When I begin to quilt, I use a hoop if the quilt is large enough. If not, I lap quilt. I like to first stabilize an area, then go within that area and do the detail quilting. Keeping the quilt as square as possible is important to the success of the piece. Be careful not to distort the quilt. When putting the quilt in a hoop, be careful not to pull the quilt too taut. Otherwise, rocking the needle when you quilt will be difficult. When the quilt top is in place and taut, place your hand, fingers spread, in the center and gently push down to give the fabric some slack.

Plan the quilting and make decisions based upon what is best for the quilt. Listen…

PREPARING THE QUILT FOR BINDING

It's important that the quilt edge is well prepared before applying the binding. I prefer to bind my quilts as soon as I can. To do that successfully, I use cotton batting so the three layers "stick" together rather than slide or slip as they might with polyester. I do some additional basting on the border edge. If the three layers flair at the edge, the binding will be difficult to apply.

Binding before quilting the border helps to define and stabilize the border area for quilting and helps prevent wavy borders. If the final border is generously wide, reestablishing 90° corners and straight sides will be easy. Position the Bias Square® similarly at each corner and draw the corners to square the quilt. Connect the corner lines to establish the sides. Align the raw edges of the binding to this line when sewing to the quilt.

To know that the corners are accurate, determine the finished border width plus ¼" seam allowance needed to apply the binding. For example, if you want to see 2" of border, you would position the Bias Square 2¼" from the last corner seam line, being sure the miter fold and the 45° line on the Bias Square were in alignment. Position the Bias Square at the last point at which your quilt had 90° corners and straight sides. When applying binding, align the raw edges to the

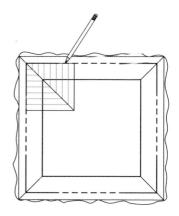

drawn line. I often sew the binding on by machine and then finish quilting before I trim the quilt and do the handwork on the back.

BINDING

Binding is the final design element and color opportunity for your quilt…give it adequate, careful consideration. Binding can add a final touch of contrasting color, or match the final border and create a smooth finish. Binding should be proportionate to the size and scale of the quilt. When working in a small scale, the total visual impact is immediate. The eye will find discrepancies quickly, so be especially careful when cutting and sewing the binding.

Binding can be cut on the straight grain or the bias. I use continuous straight grain binding most of the time. Continuous bias binding is necessary on quilts that are scalloped or have rounded corners or a zigzag edge. The bias has the most stretch and therefore conforms to curved edges easily. I sometimes use bias binding when the fabric print is more interesting on the diagonal, such as small checks or fine stripes. Use the fabrics to their full potential and take advantage of the print. Do what's best for the quilt. Mitering the corners when binding gives a tailored look as opposed to a softer look with rounded corners. We have lots of choices.

I usually make continuous double fold, straight grain binding and sew with a $1/4$" seam allowance. When the quilt is very small, I use continuous single fold, straight grain binding and sew it on with a $1/8$" seam allowance. Each project will give the specific size and amounts. Refer to a basic quiltmaking book for instructions on how to cut, make, and apply binding. I will share the method that works for me to join the binding ends smoothly.

Join the Binding Ends Smoothly—Bias or Straight Grain

1. First recreate the 45° angle that is on the beginning tail onto the ending tail, in the right place. Lay the ending tail on the quilt edge, matching raw edges. If the ending tail is too long, cut it so it lays within the allotted space.

2. Place the beginning tail (the one with the angle) inside the ending tail, smooth and flat. Where the long and short points of the beginning tail touch the ending tail, make a mark or dot. Remove the beginning tail, open the ending tail flat, and connect the two marks with any straight edge. The angle is now recreated.

3. Add seam allowance to the angle before cutting or sewing the two ends together. Draw another line $1/2$" from the first line. All the seam allowance will be on the ending tail. Cut on the line just drawn.

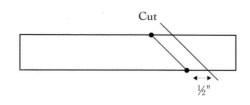

Cut

$1/2$"

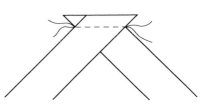

4. Sew the two tails, right sides together, with a $\frac{1}{4}$" seam allowance. Handle the ends carefully; they are bias and stretch easily. The $\frac{1}{4}$" seam allowance should have you begin sewing right at the crevice of the extended points at each end.

5. Press this seam open, then repress the fold. Sew from where you stopped stitching to where you began, pinning where necessary.

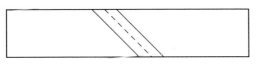

6. Bring the folded edge of binding to the back of the quilt and hand stitch in place, matching thread to binding. Create miters on the back of the quilt by folding the fabric appropriately. Hand stitch the miter folds closed.

PIPING

Piping creates a three-dimensional fine line of color right in front of the binding. Choose a fabric and color that contrasts with the binding. This area can be very bright, intense, deep, or dark. Interview until you find just the right color and fabric.

You will need the same number of inches as the binding.

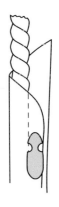

1. Using your favorite method, create a continuous bias $\frac{7}{8}$" wide.

2. Fold bias in half wrong sides together and press carefully.

3. Lay the $\frac{1}{8}$" cording inside the folded bias and sew just next to the cording, using a zipper or similar foot.

4. Work slowly, using the stiletto to keep the cording in place. Keep the edges even and the bias straight and relaxed while sewing.

BLOCKING FINISHED QUILTS

When my quilts are completely finished and bound, I carefully evaluate them to be sure corners are 90° angles and the sides are straight. If I need to make any adjustments or corrections, I pin and manipulate the quilt into shape, face down, to a soft flat surface (I use the carpeting in my sewing room). I carefully steam my quilt from the back, just skimming the iron over the fabric. Cotton batting responds well to the steam, and any problems or discrepancies are easily corrected. I am unfamiliar with blocking quilts using polyester batting. Let the quilt cool and dry in place before removing the pins. Be sure to use good quality, fine pins.

DISPLAYING SMALL SCALE WORK

The manner in which small scale quilts are displayed or presented contributes to and affects their credibility.

The *Framed Double Wedding Ring* quilt I share in this book had a different life before framing. When I would show it holding it up between my fingers just as you would show any quilt, it was often called a potholder. I began to realize that I needed to present this work in a different way so others would "see" it through my eyes and understand the joy and pleasure small scale quiltmaking offers. Putting this small quilt in a frame gives it elegance, style, charm, and credibility.

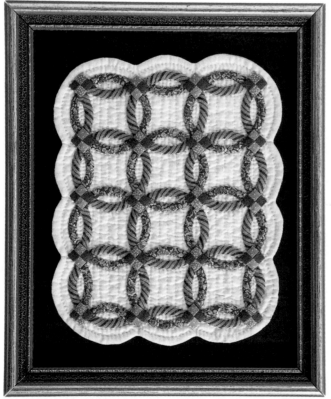

Framed Double Wedding Ring 6" x 7 1/2"

You, or a framer, can frame small quilts simply or elaborately; the choice is yours. Do what is best for the quilt. Pay attention to how art is framed and matted; get ideas and input so that if you go to a professional you have some idea of how you want it to look and/or feel. Be open to framers' expertise and suggestions. You can frame a completely bound quilt by sewing it onto a mat board, or you can frame by wrapping the final border around a form that fits into a frame, as in *Key Chain* or *Heritage*. I would encourage you to frame without glass. Viewers can get much closer and more intimate with the piece, it will be much easier to photograph, and it views more clearly and beautifully. To dust, gently brush with an artist's brush, or use a damp sponge, or carefully use masking tape to "pat" dust from the surface. Stabilize the quilt with your hand so that whatever method you use to dust does not pull the quilt away from the form. If you do use glass, use clear glass and put spacer bars at the corners so that the glass does not touch the fabric. Non-glare glass is clouded and can distort colors.

To display small, unframed quilts I sew a sleeve to the back and run a narrow dowel through it. The dowel remains behind the quilt and sits on small brads or nails at each end.

Small quilts require a small place to hang. Don't hang a single small quilt on a huge wall; it will get lost and look silly. Displaying quilts in your home creates a comfortable feeling of welcome and a softness that invites conversation.

Key Chain, 14" Square

Santa Fe, 23" Square

Pieced Double Wedding Ring, 18" x 22" and Framed Double Wedding Ring, 6" x 7¹/₂"

Shadow Baskets, 28 ¹/₂" Square

Porcelain Doll by Laurie Maas, Simi Valley, California

Heritage, 18" Square

Mosaic Mask, 18" Square and Ohio Sampler, 18" Square

THE PROJECTS

When you have chosen a project, I suggest you read the instructions completely to get a "sense" of the project and how it is assembled before you begin. The projects are presented in order of their challenge. I encourage you to take these projects and make them yours just as I did. I combined traditional blocks in new ways or with fresh colors to come up with my own creations, which then needed their own names. Although this part is difficult for me, it comes easily to my husband Joe, so he named most of these. Now it is your turn to change the set, the size, the colors. Make them reflect your own creative spirit. See these projects as a springboard for your own ideas. Have fun!

Note: Yardage requirements are usually based on ¹/₄ yard minimum cuts and therefore generous.

Key Chain, 14" Square. Machine Pieced by Author.

KEY CHAIN

The Churn Dash block is easily constructed, and is a favorite of my husband. This is a framed, unquilted project that combines one 3" Churn Dash block, windowpaned and surrounded with sixteen 1½" Churn Dash blocks. Multiple borders complete the quilt top. The construction of this quilt is easy, so focus on using many different colors, shades, and visual textures of fabric in the blocks and borders. The center 3" block should establish and state the color scheme. The surrounding

sixteen 1½" blocks reflect that scheme through fabric and color choices. In the project quilt the center block is red and teal. I expanded these colors in value and texture when choosing the fabrics for the smaller blocks. The addition of yellow, peach, purple, brown, turquoise, and blue in small amounts enhances the red and teal scheme without changing it.

The border area repeats the center block fabrics for unity.

- Quilt Size: 14" square (not including a frame)
- Block Size: 3" finished, Grid Dimension: 1"
- Block Size: 1½" finished, Grid Dimension: ½"
- Techniques Used: Rotary cutting, strip piecing, oversizing, very narrow borders

Fabric Requirements

- Background: ¼ yard
- Block Fabric: a large assortment of 5" squares in various shades, colors, and visual textures
- Windowpane Fabric: If using a border print with a template and mitered corners, you would need ¼ yard of a border print. If using a nondirectional or all over print, a 6" square would be sufficient.
- Borders: ¼ yard pieces of several choices

3" Churn Dash Block

Grid Dimension: 1"—Make One

1. Shape A: Cut two 1⅞" squares of background and block fabric, cut in half diagonally. Sew background A and block A triangles together, press stitches, press seam toward dark. Repeat to make 4 A/A units. These A/A units should measure 1½" square. Trim dog ears and seam allowance.

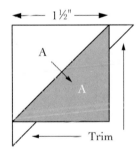

2. Shape B: Cut one 7" x 1" strip of block fabric and background fabric. Sew the strips together along one long edge with a ¼" seam allowance; press stitches, press seam toward dark fabric. Cut four 1½" segments from the B/B strip unit, keeping a vertical line of the ruler on the edge of the fabric and a horizontal line of the ruler on the seam to ensure accurately angled cuts; trim seams.

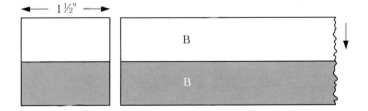

3. Shape C: Cut one 1½" square for the center.
4. On a flannel board, referring to photo and diagram, lay out the A/A units, the B/B units and C. Sew units together in each row; press seams in direction of arrows. Sew straight and accurately. Rows should measure 3½" x 1½".
5. Sew the three rows together, matching and pinning at intersections and outside edges; press seams in direction of arrows. Block should measure 3½" square. Return to flannel board.

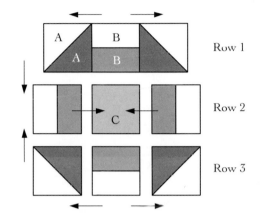

One 1½" Churn Dash Block

Grid Dimension: ½"—Make Sixteen

The D/D and E/E units will be cut and sewn oversized and then trimmed to the exact size needed.

1. Shape D: Cut four 1½" squares of background and block fabric. Draw a diagonal line on the wrong side of each light square.
2. Shape E: Cut one 1" x 5" strip of background and block fabric.
3. Shape F: Cut one 1" square.
4. Construct four 1" square D/D units using Oversize Half-Square Triangle Units technique, page 24.
5. Sew the E background and block strips right sides together down the length with an accurate ¼" seam allowance. Press stitches, press seam open, trim seam allowance on both sides.
6. Cut four 1" segments off the strip unit.
7. From these 1" segments, cut four 1" squares. Using the center seam as your reference, measure out ½" in both directions and cut. These are your E/E units.

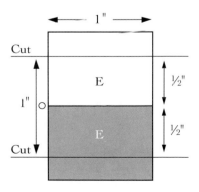

8. Lay out the entire block, evaluate, and make any needed changes.

Note: When joining units into rows, in both block sizes, sewing very straight is important, as these seams determine the height of the triangles, and inconsistencies become apparent. Evaluate your work well before trimming the seams!

9. Sew units together in each row, paying special attention to sewing straight and maintaining grid dimension. Rows should measure 2" x 1". Press seams of Rows 1 and 3 toward corners, press seams of Row 2 toward center. Trim seams.

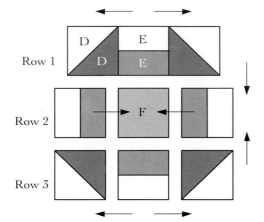

Row 1

Row 2

Row 3

10. Sew the three rows together, matching and pinning at intersections and outside edges. Press these seams toward the center. Block should measure a 2" square as you hold it in your hand. Repeat to make 16 blocks.

Note: Approximately 35 to 40 different fabrics are used to create the 16 small Churn Dash blocks in the project quilt. I share this with you not to brag, but to remind you that if you were doing this quilt full scale, and the blocks were 6", you would probably use this many fabrics easily. Don't miss out on the fun of playing with fabric. See your quilt full scale, sew small.

Windowpaning

The windowpaning design element should frame the center block and separate it from the smaller blocks. The project quilt used a border print, mitered corners, and a template. You could also use a nondirectional fabric and not miter. Both options will be offered.

Using Border Print

1. Make template G (be sure to add ¼" seam allowance to all sides). Align the center line of the template with the center of a motif in the border print, trace around the template four times, and cut. This will create smooth turning corners. Be sure to mark dots on fabric as reference marks for mitering as well. See Templates, page 25.

2. Mark a dot on the wrong side of the fabric ¼" from the edge on all four corners of the 3" Churn Dash block.

3. Pin a border print shape G to the 3" Churn Dash block; right sides together, pin at the dots and centers for proper alignment. Sew from dot to dot and backstitch. Press stitches, press seam toward windowpane. Repeat for the remaining three sides of the block.

4. Sew the four corners; begin at outside edge and sew to the dot and backstitch. Remember, do not sew into the dot, just sew close to it. Refer to Y-seam construction in the *Santa Fe* project on page 102 for further instructions. The block should now measure 5" square as you hold it in your hand.

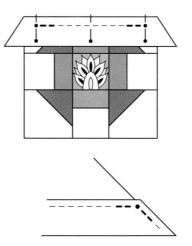

Using Nondirectional Fabric

1. Cut two 1¼" x 3½" strips of windowpaning fabric (sides).
   Cut two 1¼" x 5" strips of windowpaning fabric (top and bottom).

2. Sew the two short strips to the sides of the block, pinning and aligning edges and centers and sewing with an accurate ¼" seam allowance. Press stitches, press seam toward windowpaning. This should measure 5" x 3½". Trim seams.

3. Sew the two longer strips to the top and the bottom of the block as described in Step 2. Press stitches and press seams toward windowpaning. The block should measure 5" square as you hold it in your hand. Trim seams.

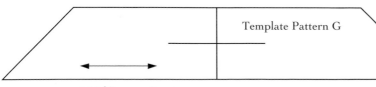

Template Pattern G

Add ¼" seam allowance

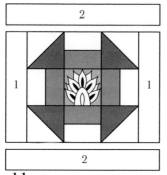

Quilt Assembly

1. Lay out the small Churn Dash blocks around the windowpaned 3" Churn Dash block, balancing color and pleasing the eye. When you have them arranged to your liking, position all the blocks so that the two long seams are all horizontal. Now turn every other one a quarter turn, which will create opposing seams for sewing. Referring to the diagram, sew Churn Dash blocks together, matching outside edges and intersections. Open seams and trim. Be attentive to the $1\frac{1}{2}$" grid dimension.

    Note: Be careful not to lose your place and forget what color went where when sewing the blocks together. Do one section at a time, keeping seam direction correct.

2. Sew two sets of three Churn Dash blocks to the sides of the 5" block. Press seams toward small blocks, trim seams.

3. Sew two sets of five Churn Dash blocks to the top and the bottom. Press seams toward the small blocks, trim seams.

4. Carefully evaluate this piece for straightness, squareness, and accuracy before adding borders. This piece should now measure an 8" square, which includes $\frac{1}{4}$" seam allowance on all sides.

Borders

Refer to Very Narrow Borders on page 35 for additional details. The total finished framed width of the border area is $3\frac{1}{8}$". The project quilt fragments that area into five individual borders. These borders are not mitered and therefore are sewn to the quilt individually by adding the two sides and then top and bottom of one fabric, then repeating that sequence for each border you add. Read the following border instructions very carefully, as this border includes two very narrow borders, which means you will be oversizing the width measurement and trimming seams. Maintain 90° corners and always sew with the quilt on top.

Border 1

1. Cut two 8" x 1" strips of appropriate fabric; sew to the sides of the quilt top, pinning at center and corners. Sew with an accurate $\frac{1}{4}$" seam allowance. Press stitches, trim the just-sewn seam allowance to an exact $\frac{1}{8}$", press seam toward Border 1.

2. Cut two 9" x 1" strips of appropriate fabric, sew to the top and bottom of the quilt top, pinning at center and corners. Sew with an accurate $\frac{1}{4}$" seam allowance. Press stitches, trim the just-sewn seam allowance to an exact $\frac{1}{8}$", press seam toward Border 1. The size of Border 1 is $\frac{3}{4}$" wide at this point. The quilt should measure 9" square.

    Note: When you add the next border, and sew next to the trimmed seam allowance, you will need to extend the sewing line as illustrated to help you identify where to begin sewing.

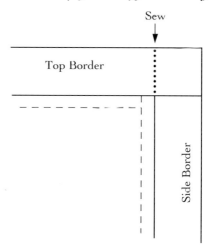

Border 2

1. Cut two 9" x $1\frac{5}{8}$" strips of appropriate fabric. Sew Border 2 to two sides of the quilt top, right sides together, quilt on top, Border 2 on the bottom. You will sew right along the cut edge of the just-trimmed seam allowance. How straight you sew this seam will determine the success of this

border. Press stitches, trim excess seam allowance to within $\frac{1}{4}$" of the last line of stitching, press toward Border 2.

2. Cut two $9\frac{3}{4}$" x $1\frac{5}{8}$" strips of appropriate fabric. Sew to the top and bottom of the quilt, right sides together, quilt on top, Border 2 on the bottom. You will sew right along the cut edge of the trimmed seam allowance. How straight you sew this seam will determine the success of this border. Press stitches, trim excess seam allowance to within $\frac{1}{4}$" of the last line of stitching, press toward Border 2. Now the finished size of Border 1 is $\frac{1}{8}$" wide and unfinished Border 2 is 1" wide. You should now have a $9\frac{3}{4}$" square.

Border 3

1. Cut two $9\frac{3}{4}$" x 1" strips of appropriate fabric, sew to the two sides of the quilt, right sides together, quilt on top, with a $\frac{1}{4}$" seam allowance, press stitches, trim seam allowance to an exact $\frac{1}{8}$", press toward Border 3.

2. Cut two $10\frac{3}{4}$" x 1" strips of appropriate fabric, sew to the top and bottom of the quilt, right sides together, quilt on top, with a $\frac{1}{4}$" seam allowance, press stitches, trim seam allowance to an exact $\frac{1}{8}$", press toward Border 3. The finished size of Border 2 is $\frac{3}{4}$" wide, and unfinished Border 3 is $\frac{3}{4}$" wide. Quilt top now measures $10\frac{3}{4}$" square.

Border 4

1. Cut two $10\frac{3}{4}$" x $1\frac{1}{4}$" strips of appropriate fabric. Sew to the sides of the quilt top, right sides together, aligning the edges of Borders 3 and 4 but sewing right along the just-trimmed edge of Border 3 seam allowance. How straight and well you sew will determine the success of this border. Press stitches, trim excess to within $\frac{1}{4}$" of the last line of stitches. Press toward Border 4.

2. Cut two $10\frac{3}{4}$" x $1\frac{1}{4}$" strips of appropriate fabric. Sew to the top and bottom of the quilt, right sides together, aligning the edges of Borders 3 and 4 but sewing right along the trimmed edge of the seam allowance. Press stitches, trim excess to within $\frac{1}{4}$" of the last line of stitches. Press seam toward Border 4. The finished size of Border 3 is $\frac{1}{8}$" wide, and unfinished Border 4 is $\frac{5}{8}$" wide. Quilt now measures $10\frac{3}{4}$" square, again! Yes, it's possible because the last seam allowance was so large.

Border 5

1. Cut two $10\frac{3}{4}$" x 3" strips of appropriate fabric. Sew to the sides of the quilt top, right sides together, quilt on top, with a $\frac{1}{4}$" seam allowance,

keeping edges of Borders 4 and 5 even. Press stitches, press seam toward Border 5.

2. Cut two $15\frac{3}{4}$" x 3" strips of appropriate fabric. Sew to the top and bottom of the quilt top, right sides together, quilt on top, with a $\frac{1}{4}$" seam allowance, keeping the edges of Borders 4 and 5 even. Press stitches, press seam toward Border 5. The finished size of Border 4 is $\frac{5}{8}$" wide, and unfinished Border 5 is $2\frac{3}{4}$" wide. The quilt should measure $15\frac{3}{4}$" square. The project quilt exposes $1\frac{3}{4}$" of the final border, so there is plenty of extra width to wrap around a form for framing if desired.

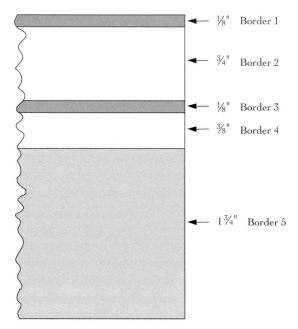

Border Finished Sizes

Steam press and block the quilt top as needed before framing. See Displaying Small Scale Quilts on page 40 for more details. The project quilt is unquilted and professionally framed without glass.

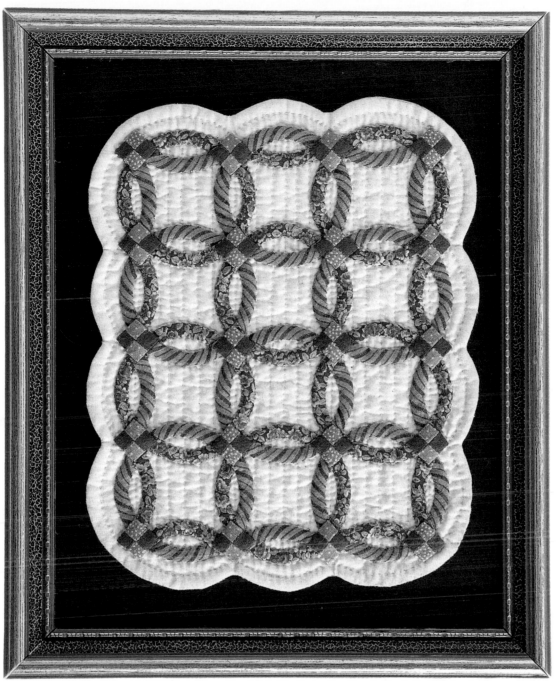

Framed Double Wedding Ring, 6" x 7 ¹/₂". Hand Appliquéd and Hand Quilted by Author.

FRAMED DOUBLE WEDDING RING

Inspiration for this charming quilt and beautiful framed gift came from Tomorrow's Heirlooms 1930s Collection. Fabric for the rings will be cut on the bias and finished ¹/₄" wide, so stripes and checks work beautifully. To help you interview fabrics, cut a ¹/₄" window in a 3" x 5" card and lay it on possible fabric choices on the bias. This gives you the opportunity to "read" the fabric before cutting.

Proportionately smaller scaled prints work best in this project. You could use one or two or more fabrics for all the rings. If you use more than one fabric for the rings, change the visual texture. Note how the project quilt brings a fine stripe and small floral together. The four patches are most successful when fabrics have low activity such as tone-on-tone or solids.

You will transfer the ring pattern onto the background fabric. Then make the bias rings and four patches by machine. The rings and four patches are then hand appliquéd in place.

Ring Pattern (See page 4 for photocopy permission.)

- Finished Quilt Size: 6" x 7$\frac{1}{2}$"
- Ring Size: 2$\frac{1}{2}$"
- Techniques Used: Bias bar, strip piecing, and framing
- Tools: $\frac{1}{4}$" metal Bias Bar™, fabric glue stick, round wooden toothpick

Fabric Requirements
- Rings: $\frac{1}{4}$ yard total
- Four Patches: $\frac{3}{4}$" x 40" strip of two fabrics
- Background: 12" square
- Backing: 12" square
- Batting: 12" square

Background

You can reduce or increase the number of rings by shifting the pattern under the background.

1. Dampen and press the background fabric well; this will be the last time you press it.
2. Trace or photocopy the ring pattern. Place the ring pattern under the background fabric and stabilize both with drafting tape. Using a lead pencil or white pencil, depending on your fabric choices, lightly and carefully trace the circles. You can also mark your quilting lines at this time if you are sure of the design you want. Set aside.

Note: A dark background would require a light box or taping to a window to transfer the pattern.

Rings

1. Cut a total of 12 bias strips, 1" x 13". Press each strip in half lengthwise, wrong sides together. Chain sew all 12 bias strips with a $1/4$" seam allowance from the fold. When you have sewn a few inches, test for accuracy by inserting the $1/4$" metal Bias Bar™ into the bias tube. It should fit snugly.
2. Insert the $1/4$" metal Bias Bar into one bias tube, trim the seam allowance, move the seam to just shy of the center.

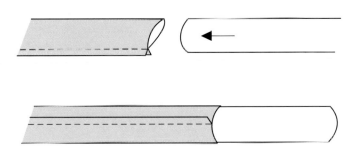

3. Lightly dampen and press with dry iron set on cotton (or steam press) both front and back, being careful not to scorch. Let the Bias Bar cool in the fabric before removing to ensure a flat, well-creased bias tube.

Note: The Bias Bar gets very hot. If you need to touch it, use a scrap of fabric as a potholder.

4. Remove the Bias Bar when cool. With raw edges of seam allowance toward the outer edge of the ring, press again while gently forming circles. Repeat for remaining bias tubes.
5. From each bias tube, cut an 8" length for a circle, and two $2^1/4$" lengths for two arcs. Using a fabric glue stick, apply glue to the back of the bias on

the seam, not on the edges. Use enough to adhere the arcs and circles securely in place. The drawn line is the outside edge of the rings. First place the 14 arcs in place around the edge of the quilt, then apply the 12 circles.

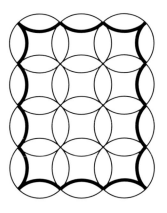

When placing the bias on the background to form the complete circles, begin and end at an intersection. Clip the ends to meet in the middle of that intersection. Position the raw edges of the seam allowance toward the outside of the circle to create a smoother curve.

Four-Patches

1. Pair the two ($3/4$" x 40") four-patch strips, right sides together, on grain and press. Cut in half (two 20" strips are easier to sew accurately than one long 40" piece). Sew down the length of both strip pairs using an accurate $1/4$" seam allowance.
2. Press stitches to set and relax them, then open the seam by combing the threads with your nail. Press with the iron and trim both sides of the seam allowance slightly. This two-strip unit should measure 1" edge to edge, or $1/2$" seam to edge.

Press open / 1"

3. Cut forty $3/4$" segments from the two strip units. To cut accurately, position a vertical line of the ruler on the edge of the fabric and a horizontal line of the ruler on the seam.

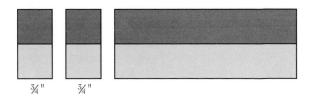

$3/4$" $3/4$"

4. Position two segments together to form a four-patch, matching and pinning the center seam and keeping the outside edges even. Sew slowly and straight. Press stitches and gently finger-press the seam open, then press with the iron. You should now have a 1" square four-patch. If you do, trim the seam allowance and repeat 19 more times. It's very important that the four-patches are accurate, that the edges are even, and that they perfectly match in the center.

5. To form ¹/₂" squares from the 1" four-patches, apply a small amount of glue from the glue stick (I use a toothpick to pick up glue and apply to fabric) to the wrong side of the four-patch at the center seam. Bring two opposite edges of the four-patch to the center seam and glue baste in place, continuing to use the toothpick to manipulate and form even edges.

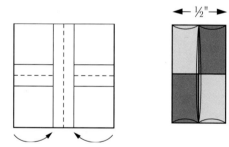

6. Apply a small amount of glue on the wrong side of the four-patch at the center seam again and bring the remaining two edges to the center, manipulating carefully to create a ¹/₂" square four-patch. Repeat 19 more times. Set aside.

Note: I find it helpful to lay the toothpick where the fold would be to give the fabric something rigid to fold over and create a more definitive straight edge.

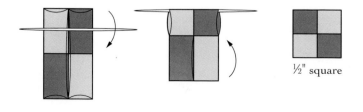

½" square

7. Hand appliqué the arcs and circles first, then glue baste the four-patches at each intersection, covering raw edges of ring ends, and hand appliqué. Always match thread color to the piece being appliquéd, not background fabric. Be sure four-patches are all positioned similarly. Because of the bulk at the four-patch area, you will probably appliqué one stitch at a time, gently tugging on the thread to nestle the four-patch down into the intersection of the rings.

Quilt Assembly

1. Mark the quilting design.
2. On the wrong side of the quilt top, mark a sewing line, ¹/₂" from the appliqué stitches, following the curves of the quilt and pivoting at the four-patch points. Notice the project quilt has curved edges only, no points!

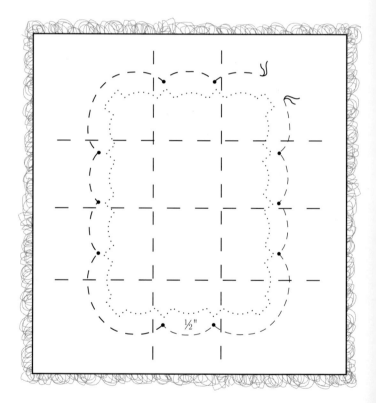

3. Because this quilt is so small, splitting the batting you usually use would be appropriate. Place the batting on the bottom, the backing next, right side up, the quilt top next, right side down, and baste the three layers together to prevent shifting while sewing around the perimeter of the quilt.
4. Sew on the drawn line, slowly, with a small stitch length and a well-blended thread color. Leave a corner curve unsewn for turning. Evaluate your sewing carefully. Trim to within ³/₁₆" of stitching,

clip curves and inside points, remove basting, turn the quilt right side out, carefully manipulating the edge of the quilt to create and form symmetrical curves. Take the time to form a pleasing, rounded edge. If you are working with light fabric be sure your hands are clean, as the oil from them can dirty the edge as you handle the fabric.

5. Hand stitch the opening closed.
6. The project quilt uses matching thread and is quilted with vertical lines, $1/4$" apart and along both sides of each ring.

Framing

This quilt fits beautifully in an 8" x 10" frame. Find one you like (no glass is needed), and have an 8" x 10" mat cut from acid-free board in a color and texture you like. Be sure to take your quilt with you when choosing the mat board color and frame.

To sew the quilt onto the mat board:

1. Center the quilt on the mat board by eye with the help of a ruler.

2. Pin the quilt to the board, positioning the pins vertically. Place two at the top and two at the bottom.
3. Leaving the pins in the quilt, remove it from the mat board. On the back of the quilt, where the four pins exit, make a mark. Remove the pins.
4. Enlarge the holes on the mat board slightly. Thread a needle with quilting thread, knot it, enter the back of the mat board into the corresponding mark on the back of the quilt, and leave a tail on the back. Sew across the back of the quilt, using basting stitches and staying in the back and batting, to the other mark, and exit the quilt, into the board, out the back, and tie the two thread ends together tightly. Secure the other end of the quilt to the mat board in the same way.

Larger quilts might require additional sewing. This is a lovely gift and a special way to give from your heart.

Mosaic Mask, 18" Square. Machine Pieced by Author. Machine Quilted by Margaret Gair of San Ramon, California.

MOSAIC MASK

This quilt is made exclusively from the entire Miniature Medley fabric collection of RJR Fashion Fabrics designed by Jinny Beyer. Other fabrics will also work well. It includes four color families (red, blue, brown, and green) plus one yellow and two background lights. Notice that the four color families are used equally, yet the border color determines the color of the quilt. I could just have easily used the blue border print and ended up with a blue quilt.

This quilt combines 37 single nine-patches with plain squares to create nine Double Nine-Patch blocks. I made two Double Nine-Patch blocks from each color,

then used all the colors in the center block.

Setting the Double Nine-Patch blocks on point creates four alternate block spaces. Each of these is dissected into four triangles and pieced from the same area of the border print four times.

The side triangle and corner areas are fragmented to create a narrow band of color that runs underneath the blocks. The border is mitered and made of multiple strips of fabric.

Again, the simplest of patterns creates a beautiful expression.

- Quilt Size: 18" Square
- Block Size: Double Nine-Patch $3^3/8$" finished, Grid Dimension: $1^1/8$"
- Block Size: Single Nine-Patch $1^1/8$" finished, Grid Dimension: $^3/8$"
- Techniques Used: Strip piecing, templates, mitering

Fabric Requirements:
- Single Nine-Patches: $^1/4$ yard each of one dark and one medium of four colors
- Shape A: Small amount of a variety of medium prints of four colors
- Shape B: $1^1/2$ yards of a border print (this includes border requirements)
- Shape C and D: $^1/4$ yard each of two light fabrics and one dark fabric
- Border 1: See Shape B
- Border 2: $^1/4$ yard of a light, bright, or intense color
- Border 3: $^1/4$ yard of a dark fabric
- Binding: 90" of 2" wide straight grain, double fold
- Backing: 22" square
- Batting: 22" square

Once you have made some fabric and color choices, separate the fabric into color piles, then into value piles (lights, mediums, and darks).

Shape A

Cut forty-four $1^5/8$" squares from medium fabrics. Five of these squares and four single nine-patch blocks make up a double nine-patch block.

Single Nine-Patches
Grid Dimension: $^3/8$"

To make this quilt as I did, you will need a total of 37 single nine-patch blocks (ten of color one, ten of color two, nine of color three, and eight of color four). The following cutting instructions will yield ten single nine-patch blocks from one pairing of color. You will repeat this three more times in the other colors.

1. Pair a dark and medium fabric, right sides together, on grain and press. Cut five $^7/8$" x 9" strips off the lengthwise grain.
2. Sew three pairs together, keeping edges even and sewing with an accurate $^1/4$" seam allowance. Press stitches, finger-press seam toward dark fabric, then press with the iron. The two strip units should measure $1^1/4$" from edge to edge. If they do, trim the seams.
3. Sew a dark strip to two units and a medium strip to one unit. Press stitches, finger-press seam in

the same direction, then press with the iron. Both seams are in the same direction. The three strip units should measure $1^5/8$" from edge to edge ($^3/8$" grid dimension). Trim seams.

$$^3/8" + ^3/8" + ^3/8" \text{ grid dimension} = ^9/8"$$
$$+^1/2" \text{ seam allowance} = ^{13}/8" = 1^5/8"$$

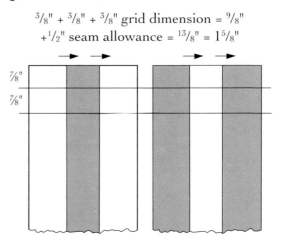

4. Cut twenty $^7/8$" segments from the dark-medium-dark strip units and ten $^7/8$" segments from the medium-dark-medium strip unit. This will make ten single nine-patch blocks.

Note: Keep both a vertical line of the ruler on the edge of your fabric, and horizontal lines of the ruler on both seams to ensure a straight right angle.

5. Pair a segment from each unit, arranging the segments to create opposing seams, keeping edges even and intersections snugly matched and pinned. Chain sew the pairs straight and slowly with an accurate $^1/4$" seam allowance. Press stitches, finger-press seam in one direction, then press with the iron. Manipulate and arrange with your hands to keep the unit straight, rectangular, and unbowed. This two-segment unit should measure $1^5/8$" x $1^1/4$". Trim seams.

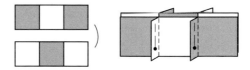

6. Add the remaining ten segments in the same way. Press seams in the same direction. The single nine-patch blocks should measure $1^5/8$". Trim seams.

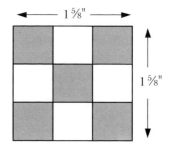

Double Nine-Patches

Grid Dimension: $1^1/8$"

1. On a flannel board, lay out the single nine-patch blocks and the Shape A $1^5/8$" squares to create the interior area of the quilt. Play with their placement and arrange to your satisfaction.

2. Sew nine double nine-patch blocks together, following diagram and pressing path. Double nine-patch block should measure $3^7/8$" square. Place the blocks back on the flannel board.

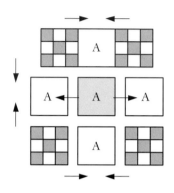

Alternate Block

1. The alternate block is a square on point divided into quarters diagonally. Make a template for Shape B. Refer to Templates on page 25. Cut 16 from a border print.

2. To interview fabric, place template B on the right side of the border print. Place the taped mirrors on the sewing line, slide the template out, and leave the mirrors in place to reflect how the alternate block would look. Move the template and mirrors around the border print, interviewing different designs until you find just the right one. Make reference marks on the right side of the template so you can locate the same place on the fabric again. Position the template right side up on the right side of the border print, using the reference marks as your guide. Trace around the template four times for each alternate block design. Cut out the shapes and position on the flannel board.

Note: Grain arrow placement is preferred; however, move the template freely while interviewing and be flexible. If you decide to cut your shapes off grain, just handle and sew them carefully.

3. Sew the Shape B triangles together to form four $3^7/8$" squares. Press to create opposing seams.

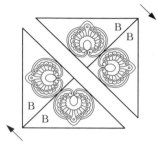

4. Place the alternate blocks on the flannel board.

Pieced Side Triangles and Corners

Make templates for Shapes C and D, transferring all markings. Shapes C and D create the pieced side triangles and corners. They include three different fabrics (two light, one dark) that are sewn together, and then a template is placed on the strip unit, matching reference lines. You then trace around the template and cut.

1. Cut two $2^1/2$" x 40" strips of light (large triangle area).
   Cut two $3/4$" x 40" strips of dark (narrow band).
   Cut two $1^1/2$" x 40" strips of second light fabric (outer edge of Shapes C and D).

2. Make two appropriate strip units, sewing the strips together very straight, keeping edges even, and sewing with an accurate $1/4$" seam allowance. Press the stitches, press seam allowances away from narrow band.

3. Place templates face down on the wrong side of the strip unit, matching reference lines on template to stitching lines. If lines and stitches do not match exactly, align one line on the template to the same stitching line consistently. Cut eight from Template C (side triangles). Cut eight from Template D (corners).

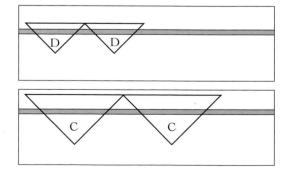

4. Piece two D shapes together, four times, to create corners, matching intersections well so narrow band turns the corner smoothly.

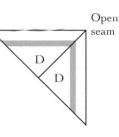

Open seam

5. Place side triangles and corners on the flannel board. Evaluate and make any changes necessary.

Quilt Assembly

1. Sew quilt top together in diagonal rows, pressing seams away from the Double Nine-Patch blocks.

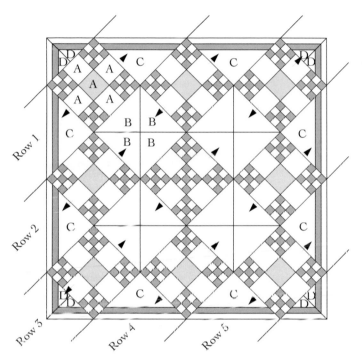

2. Join rows one through five, matching intersections and outside edges. Press after adding each row. Add corners last. Press well with steam, keeping the quilt top square.

Borders

The border area is $3\frac{1}{2}$" wide and then fragmented into three different widths of three different fabrics. I divided the area up, letting the width of the border print be my guide. Try different combinations until you find the right one for your quilt.

Note: Remember to position the same motif of the border print at the center of each side of the quilt to create smooth, well-matched corners on a square quilt. Refer to Mitering Corners by Hand, and Border Prints with Mitered Corners, page 34.

- Border 1: Cut four strips $2\frac{1}{8}$" x 25" from the border print ($1\frac{5}{8}$" finished).
- Border 2: Cut four strips $\frac{7}{8}$" x 25" from light, bright, or intense color ($\frac{3}{8}$" finished).
- Border 3: Cut four strips $2\frac{1}{2}$" x 25" from dark color. This is a generous width to allow for straightening any distortion that may occur during quilting.

Join the three border strips four times. Sew the borders to the quilt top and miter, creating 90° corners. Layer, baste, and quilt. See Preparing the Quilt for Binding, page 37. The finished width of Border 3 on the project quilt measures $1\frac{5}{8}$" plus $\frac{1}{4}$" for binding space ($1\frac{7}{8}$" total). I used 2" doublefold binding cut on the straight grain with mitered corners. Refer to Binding, page 38.

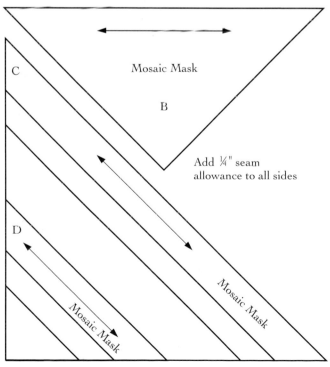

C

Mosaic Mask

B

Add $\frac{1}{4}$" seam allowance to all sides

D

Mosaic Mask

Mosaic Mask

Heritage, 18" Square. Hand Appliquéd and Hand Quilted by Author.

Appliqué is the process of applying shapes onto a background area by hand or machine. I have always admired the beautiful and intricate quilts that demonstrate this technique. Working in a smaller scale allows me to experience the joy of hand appliqué without taking up as much time as a full size quilt would.

I wanted a very classic, traditional feeling piece, so I combined red and green flowers and leaves with a

HERITAGE

light background developed in layers: a circle, an eight-sided shape, and a square. Creating a difference in both the visual texture and shade between the three shapes gives added interest, dimension, and detail. The background should be interesting but subtle, as the appliqué wreath and corners are the primary focus. The borders should enhance your appliqué and bring it to a beautiful conclusion.

- Finished Quilt Size: 18" square (exposed in the frame)
- Techniques Used: Freezer paper/glue tube, embroidery, multiple strip borders with mitered corners, very narrow borders, bias bar, English paper piecing, trapunto
- Tools: GluTube®, glue stick, Hot Tape™, tweezers, toothpick, utility scissors, freezer paper, typing-weight paper, tapestry needle, small amount of yarn, dental floss threader, compass, $\frac{1}{8}$" metal Bias Bar™, and sandpaper board

Fabric Requirements:

- Background: three different background fabrics that vary subtly in print and shade
- Shape 1—6" square
- Shape 2—10" square
- Shape 3—$12\frac{3}{4}$" square
- Leaves: Small amounts of several different green prints
- Flowers: Small amounts of several strong colored, low activity prints
- Bias: $\frac{7}{8}$" x 37" unseamed strip (a 26" square yields approximately 37" of unseamed bias)
- Border 1: $\frac{1}{4}$ yard
- Border 2: $\frac{1}{4}$ yard
- Border 3: $\frac{1}{2}$ yard
- Batting: 24" square
- Backing: 24" square—must be a fabric that allows you to see the quilting stitches in order to trapunto

Line Drawing

Note: To prepare Shapes 1, 2, and 3, as well as the leaves, I used Quilters' GluTube. This product is neat and tidy to use and enabled me to work very small successfully. It remains tacky so you can lift the fabric from the paper and reposition it if necessary. I do not know how this product might affect the fabric over time. Practice using the glue on a scrap, to get a feel for how it releases, before using on the quilt. Read the package directions completely before using.

Shape 1

1. Cut a 6" square of freezer paper, fold into quarters to determine the center and to develop horizontal and vertical fold lines to help future placement. Open up the square, dull side up. Place the compass point at the center and extend the arm $2\frac{3}{4}$" and draw a $5\frac{1}{2}$" circle.
2. Cut out the circle and iron, shiny side down, on the wrong side of the Shape 1 background fabric (6" square).
3. Apply GluTube to edges of the paper and fabric, about a scant $\frac{1}{4}$" on each. Let the glue dry.

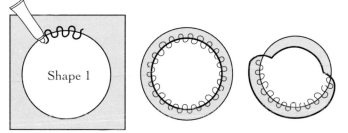

4. Cut fabric to a scant $\frac{1}{4}$" from the paper edge and bring fabric over paper edge smoothly.

Shape 2

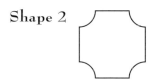

1. Cut a 10" square from freezer paper, fold into quarters as described for Shape 1. Open the square and place it, dull side up, over the pattern (page 67), aligning center, vertical, and horizontal lines to folds and center of paper. Trace one quarter of Shape 2, rotate, realign, and trace three more times to complete Shape 2. (Also trace Shape 1 as a guide to help remove paper and fabric in Background Assembly, Step 2.)
2. Cut out Shape 2 and iron, shiny side down, onto the wrong side of the Shape 2 background fabric (10" square).

3. Apply GluTube® to the edge of the paper and fabric both, about a scant ¼" on each. Let dry.

4. Cut fabric to a scant ¼" from paper edge and bring fabric over paper edge smoothly. Bring the four straight edges over first, then clip curves and bring curved edges over the paper edge. Be attentive to creating sameness on all eight corner points.

Shape 3

1. Fold Shape 3 background fabric (12³/₄" square) into quarters and crease to determine center and to develop horizontal and vertical fold lines for future placement.

2. Place a corner of Shape 3 right side up on the sandpaper board and mark the appliqué placement lines 1³/₈" in from both edges and 4" long. Repeat for the remaining three corners. The sandpaper will grip the fabric and prevent it from slipping while marking.

Background Assembly

1. Position Shape 1 onto Shape 2, aligning centers and fold lines. Thread baste or Hot Tape™ in place and appliqué using well-matched thread and tiny stitches. Remove basting or Hot Tape.

2. Turn Shape 1-2 over and carefully cut out and remove Shape 2 paper and fabric in a circle a little smaller than Shape 1. Shape 1 paper is now exposed. Carefully remove Shape 1 paper.

Note: Some paper remains in Shape 2 at the outer edge until it is appliquéd to Shape 3. Doing this helps to maintain sharp corners and smooth edges.

3. Position Shape 1–2 onto Shape 3, matching and aligning centers and fold lines. Thread baste or Hot Tape in place and appliqué, taking care that Shape 1–2 does not shift out of alignment. It's very important that Shape 1–2 remain square to Shape 3. Remove basting or Hot Tape.

4. Turn Shape 1–2–3 over, cut and remove Shape 3 fabric to within a scant ¼" of the stitches. Remove the remaining paper from Shape 2.

5. Place the assembled background face down on a soft surface and press carefully.

Borders

I have added three mitered borders to the three-layer background before adding the flowers and leaves.

The finished width of the borders are ³/₈", ¹/₈" and 2". Refer to Very Narrow Borders on page 35.

1. If your fabric is not 44", cut four strips of each border fabric at least 22" long by the appropriate width.
   - Border 1: Cut two strips ⁷/₈" x 44".
   - Border 2: Cut two strips 1" x 44". This will be the narrow ¹/₈" border.
   - Border 3: Cut two strips 4" x 44".

2. Press Border 1 to Border 2, right sides together, carefully matching raw edges and resting one fabric onto the other squarely. Sew these two strips together with an accurate ¼" seam allowance.

3. Press the stitches and then carefully and accurately trim the ¼" seam allowance to ¹/₈". Use an accurate ¹/₈" guide and rotary cut or scissor cut as desired. Then press the seam toward Border 2 from the right side of the fabric. Keep the strip unit straight.

4. Press Border 3 to Border 1–2, matching raw edges. Sew the borders together, keeping Border 1–2 on top and sewing right next to the trimmed edge of the previously sewn seam allowance. Press the stitches and then trim the excess seam allowance ¼" from the last line of stitching. Press seam toward Border 3. Border 3 remains generously wide, as it will wrap around a form and serve as a mat when framing. The project quilt exposes 2" of Border 3 after framing.

5. Repeat for remaining border strips.

6. If the border units are 44" long, cut them in half.

7. Add the four borders to the quilt top and miter the corners by hand referring to page 34.

Embroidery

Using a simple stem stitch and two strands of green embroidery floss, embroider around Shape 1 and the four corner vines. Do not embroider the tendrils until the appliqué is complete.

Outlining Shape 2 with ¹/₈" Bias

To create this ¹/₈" piece of bias use metal Bias Bars™. They make a flatter piece with sharper edges.

1. Cut one ⁷/₈" x 37" long strip of bias. It is helpful to have this be one unseamed piece, as seams will create some difficulty when inserting the metal Bias Bar.

2. Fold the bias strip in half lengthwise, wrong sides together, and gently press.

3. Sew ¼" from raw edges down the length. After a few inches are sewn, insert bar to be sure it fits snugly, but not too tight. Make any seam allowance adjustment at this time, if needed.

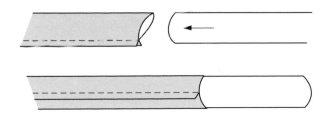

4. Trim seam to a scant $^1/_8$" and insert metal Bias Bar™. Move seam to just off center of bar. There should not be any overhang of the seam allowance.

5. Dampen seam and press with hot dry iron, being careful not to scorch. Iron dry from the back and front. To get a flat, well-creased piece of bias, let the metal Bias Bar cool in place. Advance the Bias Bar and repeat this process until the entire length of bias is prepared.

6. Using the glue stick and a toothpick, not the GluTube®, apply glue to the bias seam only and glue baste the bias to the edge of Shape 2, creating sameness on all eight corner points. Begin by folding under the raw edge and then continue to position the bias around Shape 2. When you reach the starting point, trim the bias and fold the raw edges under and align with the beginning fold.

7. When you have the bias glue-basted in place, position your work vertically. Carefully examine and evaluate for symmetry at the eight corner points. Make any adjustments necessary.

8. Appliqué the bias in place on both sides, matching thread to the bias and taking tiny stitches.

Leaves

You will need 107 leaves. To create interest and add detail, use an assortment of greens in varied scales and shades. The project quilt uses approximately 20 different green fabrics. You can either prepare all the leaves at one time or prepare them as you need them.

1. Trace or photocopy 107 leaves (page 69) onto dull side of freezer paper and cut out each leaf. You could trace half that many, or a quarter, and fold the freezer paper to multiple cut if you choose. Just be sure all your leaves are the same size and shape.

2. Place leaves, shiny side down, onto wrong side of chosen fabric(s), allowing about a $1^1/_2$" space for each leaf. Press each leaf with a dry iron to adhere paper to fabric.

3. Apply the GluTube on both fabric and paper, about $^1/_8$" to $^3/_{16}$" on each.

4. Let the glue dry. It will remain tacky.

5. Cut fabric around paper shape leaving $^1/_8$" to $^3/_{16}$" seam allowance on all sides.

6. With paper facing you, bring fabric over paper edge, creating a smooth edge and sharp points.

7. Store prepared leaves in a zippered baggie.

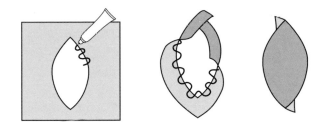

Flowers

The two sizes of flowers are made from seven hexagon shapes each. There are four large flowers at the corners and the circle wreath holds one large and two small, for a total of seven flowers. The method I use to create these flowers is the English paper method (no freezer paper and no glue).

1. Accurately trace or photocopy 35 large and 14 small hexagons (page 68) onto typing-weight paper and cut out, being sure all are the same. Take your time to do this.

2. Cut a total of 49 one-inch squares of appropriate flower fabrics. Each flower has six petals and one center.

3. Lay the paper shapes onto the wrong side of the flower fabrics and baste in place with one or two stitches, leaving the knot on the right side of the flower. Leave the needle threaded and cut the fabric around the shape leaving a $^3/_{16}$" seam allowance.

4. With paper shape facing you, bring fabric seam allowance over one edge of paper, finger crease, and baste in place. Work around the hexagon using the illustration as a guide.

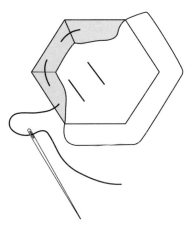

5. When you have all 49 paper hexagons covered with fabric, assemble into individual flowers. Join the hexagons by hand, sewing with an overcast

stitch, and always sewing with right sides together. Take very tiny stitches, matching thread as best you can. When all seven hexagons are sewn together to form the flower, you may remove the basting and paper from the center only. The other papers will be removed after they are appliquéd in place.

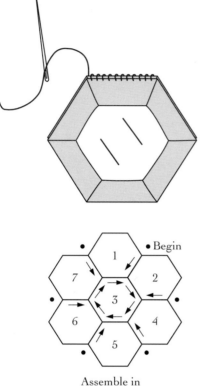

Assemble in
numerical order

Appliqué

Referring to the line drawing, position the leaves and flowers in place. Work on the center wreath first, then the corners. Hot Tape™ the leaves and flowers in place to appliqué. You could also thread baste them in place. The areas where leaves are either under or over the flower require special attention. The shape closest to the background is appliquéd first.

1. Appliqué the leaves and flowers in place with thread that matches the leaf or flower. Take small, even stitches.
2. When appliqué is complete, turn piece over and remove the paper by cutting away the background fabric to within $3/16$" of stitches. Lift fabric from paper edge with toothpick and remove paper shape carefully with tweezers, tugging gently when necessary. Always hold onto the stitches when tugging the paper.
3. Referring to the line drawing again, draw tendrils onto the background. Use one strand of embroidery floss to embroider tendrils with a simple stem stitch.

Quilting

I would encourage you to mark all quilting lines and the feather wreath before basting. The amount of quilting on this design plays an enormous role in its beauty. I used contrasting thread to define the feather wreath, and matching thread in the other areas. Because the design is appliquéd and has soft edges, I chose straight-line quilting in most areas to display the appliqué at its best. The feather wreath fills the center area, especially after it is trapuntoed.

1. The inside of the feather wreath has vertical lines $1/8$" apart.
2. The outside of the feather wreath has vertical lines $1/4$" apart.
3. Shape 2 is echo quilted by eye, using approximately $1/8$" between the lines.
4. Shape 3 is quilted with vertical lines $3/8$" apart.
5. The border area is seam quilted and then follows the print of the fabric. Quilt beyond what will be seen in the frame.

Trapunto

A backing fabric on the quilt that allows you to see clearly the feather wreath quilting stitches on the back is a must. You will trapunto from the back once the design is completely quilted. Use a tapestry needle with a blunt end and large eye and regular acrylic yarn to do the trapunto. Use a dental floss threader to thread the needle easily with the yarn. Fill each feather, referring to the illustration.

A toothpick is helpful to stuff the end of the yarn into the feather after trimming. This method of stuffing from the back is effective and easy. Laying the strands of yarn between the backing and the batting pushes the batting forward to fill the area.

Your design is now ready for framing. Frame yourself or go to a professional framer. You must also decide whether or not to put glass over the design. If you do, use clear glass only, and leave a space between the glass and the fabric.

Patterns

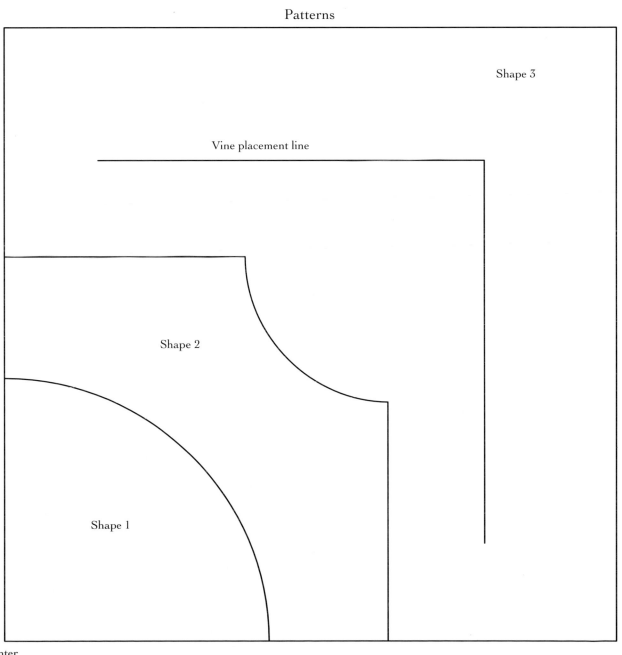

Shape 3

Vine placement line

Shape 2

Shape 1

Center

Flower Shapes

(See page 4 for photocopy permission.)

Leaf Shapes

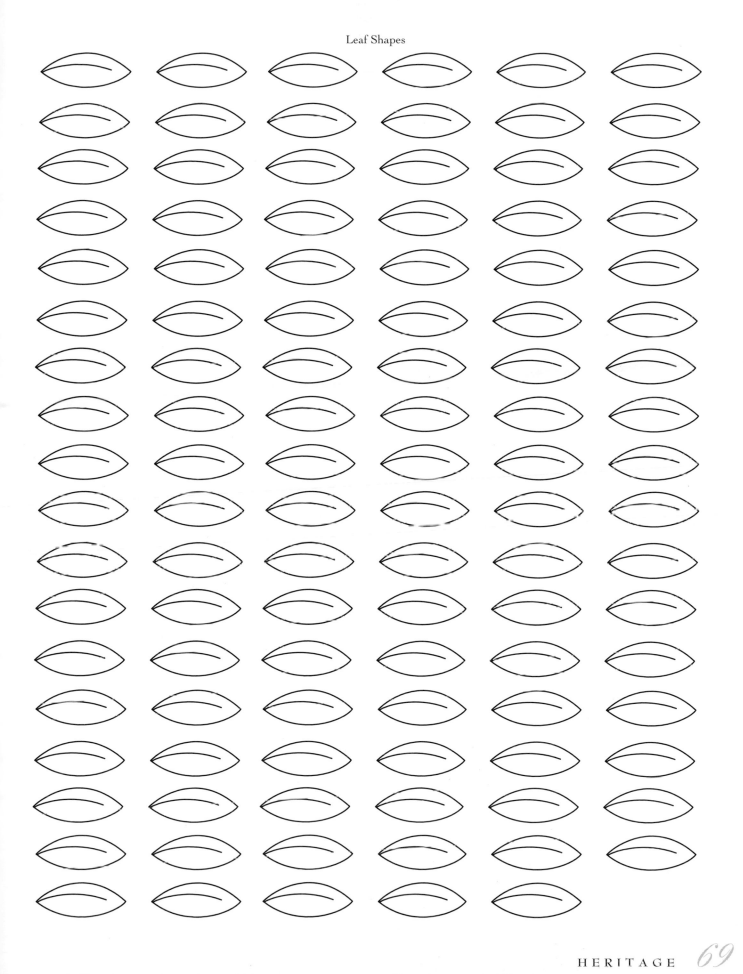

Ohio Sampler, 18" Square. Machine Pieced and Hand Quilted by Author.

OHIO SAMPLER

This quilt places five 3" sampler blocks in the corners and center of a 9" Ohio Star block. An eight-sided design element and multiple mitered borders complete the design.

Accuracy of the individual blocks will impact on the final overall appearance of the quilt. Each block should measure $3\frac{1}{2}$" as you hold it in your hand, and includes $\frac{1}{4}$" seam allowance on all four sides.

Take your time; this is not a production line, chain-piecing type of quilt. I have given you a grid dimension where appropriate, so you can measure and check your work for accuracy before trimming seams. Make each block the best it can be with regard to fabric selection, color, balance, and workmanship. Think of this quilt as if it were full size and give each block that same attention to detail.

- Finished Size: Approximately 18" Square.
- Sampler Block Size: 3" finished
- Techniques Used: English paper piecing, hand appliqué, half-square triangle—bias strip method, rotary cutting, templates, double half-square triangles, mitering
- Tools: template plastic, utility scissors, $^1/_{16}$" hole punch or large needle, freezer paper, Hot tape™.

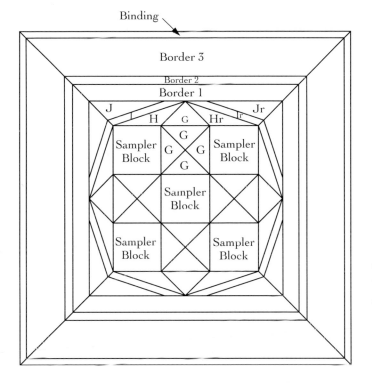

Fabric Requirements:

You will need small amounts of a variety of fabrics. You would use many different fabrics if you were making a large sampler quilt; do the same for this quilt. Vary the shade of individual colors and the visual texture of the fabrics. Use the photo for reference.

- Sampler Blocks Design Area: Small amounts of several fabrics
- Sampler Blocks Background: $^1/_4$ yard total
- Ohio Star Background: $^1/_4$ yard light
- Ohio Star Points: $^1/_4$ yard medium to dark
- Eight Sided Design Element: $^1/_4$ yard total
- Border 1: $^1/_4$ yard
- Border 2: $^1/_4$ yard
- Border 3: $^1/_4$ yard
- Binding: 90" of 2" wide straight grain, double fold
- Batting: 22" square
- Backing: 22" square

Tumbling Blocks

- Finished Block Size: 3"
- Techniques Used: English paper piecing, hand appliqué

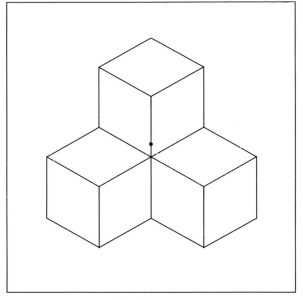

Block Diagram

Choose a light, medium, and dark of three different colors, varying the print. Consistent placement of the light, medium, and dark fabrics creates the illusion of dimension.

1. Trace and cut nine diamond shapes from the block diagram, using freezer paper.
2. Iron onto fabrics, shiny side down on wrong side of fabric, allowing a generous seam allowance.
3. Trim the fabric to $^3/_{16}$" from paper edge. Thread a needle with light quilting thread. Draw the fabric over the paper edge and baste in place on all four sides of the diamond. The wings at both points will be tucked under when the diamonds are sewn together.
4. Align one diamond onto the other as "squarely" as possible. Sew edges together by hand, using a tiny overcast stitch and well-matched thread. When you come to the end of the line, join the next diamond and continue sewing with the same threaded needle. Sew in the direction of the arrows. Repeat twice more.

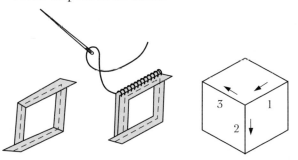

5. Join the three units together to complete the design.
6. Cut a 4" square of background fabric. Center Tumbling Blocks onto the square by folding the square into quarters to determine the center. Push a pin through the center of the Tumbling Blocks (indicated by dot on pattern) and into the center of the background square using the fold lines as guides. Baste or Hot Tape™ in place.
7. Appliqué Tumbling Blocks in place using well-matched thread and a small appliqué stitch. Remove all basting. Cut out the back of the block to within $3/16$" of stitches. Loosen and remove paper carefully with tweezers, always holding the stitches as you gently tug the paper out.
8. Press from the back and trim block to a $3^{1}/_{2}$" square.

Emiko's Lace Star
- Finished Block Size: 3"
- Techniques Used: Templates

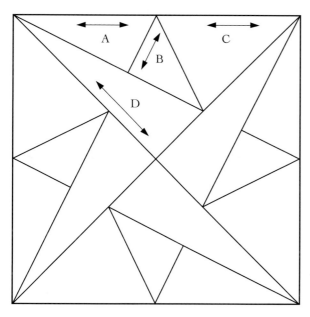

Block Diagram

Make a template for all shapes (A,B,C,D) from block diagram. Add $1/4$" seam allowance to all sides of each shape. See Templates page 25.

1. Shape A: Cut 4 from background fabric.
   Shape B: Cut 4 from star fabric.
   Shape C: Cut 4 from background fabric.
   Shape D: Cut 4 from star fabric.

Note: Marking the dots and then pinning at the dots to align the shapes onto one another "squarely" will help keep this block square. Sew from edge to edge however, not from dot to dot.

2. Lay out the block and evaluate to be sure the fabrics and colors are working. Make any changes you think are necessary, don't settle!
3. Sew A to B, right sides together, from edge to edge. Press seam toward A and trim.
4. Sew C to AB unit, right sides together, press toward C and trim.
5. Sew D to ABC unit, right sides together, press toward D and trim.
6. Repeat 3 through 5 three times.
7. Sew two ABCD units together, press seams in direction of arrows and trim. Repeat.
8. Join two halves together, matching diagonal seams and center. Sew from edge to edge, press seam open. The block should measure $3^{1}/_{2}$" as you hold it in your hand.

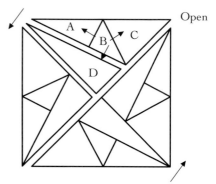

Arizona (Variation)
- Finished Block Size: 3", Grid dimension: $1/2$"
- Techniques Used: Rotary cutting, double half-square triangle and half-square triangle—bias strip method

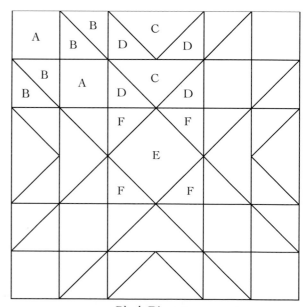

Block Diagram

Note: Evaluate the block and decide the value placement before beginning. This block is comprised of three units.

Cutting

- Shape A: Cut four 1" squares of background fabric. Cut four 1" squares of block fabric.
- Shape B: Pairs of B's will be made using the bias strip method.
- Shape C: Cut four 1" x 1¹⁄₂" rectangles of background fabric. Cut four 1" x 1¹⁄₂" rectangles of block fabric.
- Shape D: Cut sixteen 1" squares of block fabric, draw a diagonal line on the wrong side of each.
- Shape E: Cut one 1¹⁄₂" square of block fabric.
- Shape F: Cut four 1" squares of block fabric, draw diagonal line on the wrong side of each.

Unit 1:
Pairs of B's
(Bias Strip
Method)

1. Cut one 1¹⁄₂" x 20" bias strip from block fabric. Cut one 1¹⁄₂" x 20" bias strip from background fabric.
2. Follow Half-Square Triangle Units—Bias Strip Method, page 22. Sew each block fabric strip to a background strip.
3. Cut eight 1" squares from the bias strip unit. These squares are used in Unit 1 only.

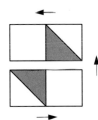

Unit 2:
Double
Half-Square
Triangles

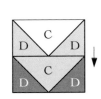

Refer to Double Half-Square Triangles, page 24. Make eight Unit 2 using fabrics chosen for Shapes C and D.

Note: Sew just on the scrap side of the diagonal line to allow 1-2 more threads of space to help the corners meet well.

Unit 3

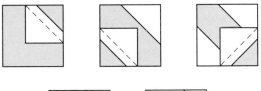

Add the F squares to the E square, right sides together, as illustrated. Trim away only the F triangles; the E square remains in place. Sewing just on the scrap side of the diagonal line helps here too!

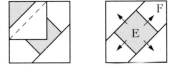

Block Assembly

Lay out the block in front of you and examine carefully. Make any changes necessary.

Sew pieces into units, units into rows, then sew rows to complete the block, matching and pinning intersections, outside edges and points. Trim as you sew, if accurate. Units should measure 1¹⁄₂" square, rows should measure 1¹⁄₂" x 3¹⁄₂" and the completed block should measure 3¹⁄₂" as you hold it in your hand.

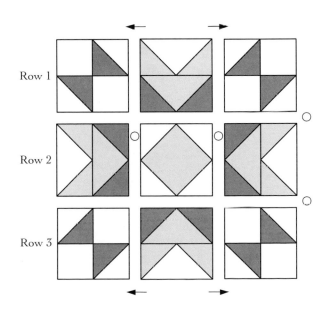

Row 1

Row 2

Row 3

Log Cabin

- Finished Block Size: 1½" (it will take four blocks to complete the 3" finished design), Grid dimension: ¼"
- Techniques Used: Straight strip sewing, rotary cutting

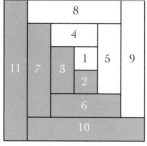

Block Diagram

1. Choose five light fabrics and six dark. Cut one ¾" x 9" (approximately) strip of each fabric. Arrange the strips in numerical order.

2. Sew Fabric 1 and 2 together lengthwise, right sides together, with an accurate ¼" seam allowance. To help keep edges aligned, it is sometimes helpful to press the two strips together before sewing.

3. Press stitches, then press seam toward Fabric 2; trim. This two-strip unit should measure 1" across.

4. Cut four ¾" segments from the two-strip unit, using lines on the ruler to help line up with seam lines. The success of this block depends on the squareness of the center, so be sure to cut and then sew very accurately.

5. Place Fabric 3 (dark) strip right side up, close to your sewing machine needle, and place a 1–2 segment, right side down, onto Fabric 3 strip. Position segment so that the seam allowance is toward you and the edges are matched. Sew very slowly and straight, with an accurate ¼" 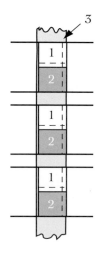 seam allowance, using a stiletto, or similar tool to help guide the pieces. Sew completely off the end of a segment before placing the next one down for sewing. Continue until all segments have been sewn onto the strip.

6. Remove from the machine and press the stitches. Cut new segments, lining up lines on ruler with edges and sewing lines. Trim seams and press seam allowance to Fabric 3. This unit should now measure 1" square.

7. Pick up Fabric 4 (light) and place it right side up near the sewing machine needle. Place 1–2–3 segments, right side down, onto Fabric 4, positioned so that the last strip added is closest to you and the seam allowance is toward you. This positioning is necessary throughout the block. Sew with an accurate ¼" seam allowance.

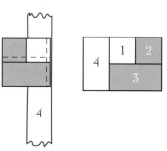

8. Continue cutting, pressing, and sewing segments in the same manner as described above. Add strips in numerical order. Measure as you sew. Remember you are working in a ¼" grid, so just add up the number of grid spaces sewn, multiply by ¼", and add ½" for seam allowance. Stay accurate. One block should measure a 2" square as you hold it in your hand (1½" finished plus ½" for seam allowance).

9. Lay out the four blocks in front of you, moving them around until you find a pleasing arrangement.

10. Sew two blocks together to form row 1. Repeat for row 2. Press seams in direction of arrows.

11. Sew rows 1 and 2 together, matching outside edges and center intersection. Press seam open or collapse; block should now measure 3½" square as you hold it in your hand.

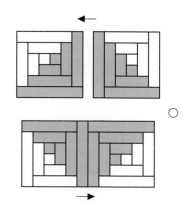

Ohio Star

- Finished Block Size: 3", Grid dimension: 1"
- Techniques Used: Rotary cutting

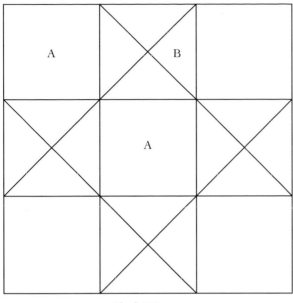

Block Diagram

1. Shape A: Cut four $1^1/_2$" squares of background fabric for corners. Cut one $1^1/_2$" square of block fabric for center.

   Shape B: Cut three $2^1/_4$" squares of block fabric, cut in quarters diagonally. Cut one $2^1/_4$" square of background fabric, cut in quarters diagonally.

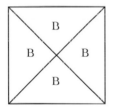

2. Join four B triangles to create Unit 1. Arrows indicate pressing direction. Repeat three more times.

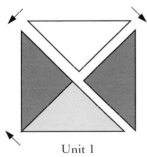

Unit 1

3. Lay out block and assemble Row l, measuring as you sew, pinning when necessary, pressing in direction of arrows and trimming seams. Each row, individually, should measure $1^1/_2$" x $3^1/_2$".

4. Assemble Rows 2 and 3.
5. Join rows, pinning at outside edges and at intersections. Measure as you sew, press in direction of arrows, and trim seams. Block should measure $3^1/_2$" as you hold it in your hand.

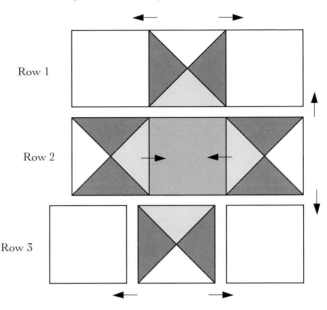

Row 1

Row 2

Row 3

9" Ohio Star Set Block

The five $3^1/_2$" sampler blocks will now be set into the center and corner positions.

Cutting

1. Shape G: Cut three $4^1/_4$" squares of light fabric, cut into quarters, diagonally. (Eight are needed in the 9" Ohio Star, and four will be used in the eight-sided design element that surrounds the 9" Ohio Star).
2. Cut two $4^1/_4$" squares of medium to dark fabric, cut into quarters, diagonally. This fabric defines the Ohio Star design and plays a dominant role in the quilt. Choose a low activity fabric that does not distract from the sampler blocks.

Star Point Assembly

1. Lay out the G triangles and the sampler blocks to create the Ohio Star and evaluate for color and strength.
2. Sew four G triangles together as illustrated, pressing in direction of arrows. Do not trim seams. This should measure $3^1/_2$" square as you hold it in your hand. Repeat three times.

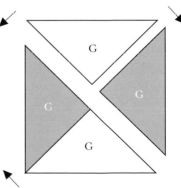

9" Ohio Star Assembly

1. Lay out sampler blocks and Star Points to create the Ohio Star. Position the five sampler blocks so that they are balanced in color and pleasing to the eye.

2. Sew sampler blocks and Star Points together to form three rows. Each row should measure $3\frac{1}{2}$" x $9\frac{1}{2}$".

3. Join Rows 1, 2, and 3 together, matching outside edges and intersections and pressing in the direction of the arrows. Block now measures $9\frac{1}{2}$" square.

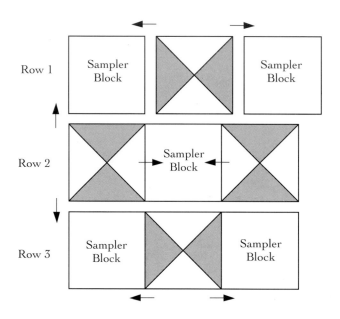

Eight-Sided Design Element

The $9\frac{1}{2}$" Ohio Star block will now be surrounded by an eight-sided design element. Refer to page 25 for specifics on making accurate templates for shapes H, I, and J. Shape G has been cut previously. When tracing around the template shapes on the wrong side of your fabric, be sure to mark the dots; they will help you to align shapes for sewing. You will sew from edge to edge.

1. Cut four H and four H reverse (reverse means turn template over).
   Cut four I and four I reverse.
   Cut four J and four J reverse.

2. Sew four HIJ units and four HrIrJr units, matching and pinning at dots. Press in direction of arrows.

3. Lay out one HIJ unit and one HrIrJr unit with a G triangle in between. Sew as illustrated and press in direction of arrows. Repeat three more times.

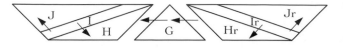

4. Add these four units to each side of the $9\frac{1}{2}$" Ohio Star block, starting and stopping $\frac{1}{4}$" from the edge and backstitch. Press toward outside edge.

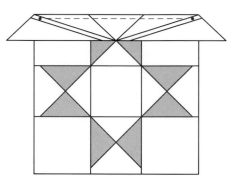

5. Sew the four corners closed, starting at the outside edge, stopping at the dot and backstitch. Press this seam all to one side.

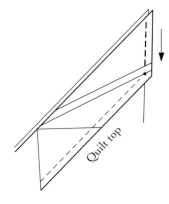

6. You now have a $12\frac{1}{2}$" block.

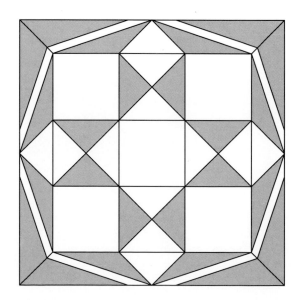

Borders

To decide on three border fabrics I usually pull and interview many more than that so I have many choices. These borders should enhance the quilt and make it better than it is without one. The visual texture of Borders 1 and 3 add interest and the dark, narrow Border 2 separates, outlines, and defines.

- Border 1: Cut four strips $1^{1}/_{2}"$ x 22". (If using a border print, remember to place the same area or motif of the fabric at the center of all four sides of the quilt to create smoothly turned corners.)
- Border 2: Cut four strips, $^{3}/_{4}"$ x 22".
- Border 3: Cut four strips $2^{3}/_{4}"$ x 22".

The border is mitered at the corners so all three fabrics can be sewn together and added to the quilt top as one.

1. Press a Border 1 strip to a Border 2 strip, right sides together, aligning raw edges and registering the two fabrics onto one another. Sew down the length with an accurate $^{1}/_{4}"$ seam allowance.
2. Press stitches, then press seam allowance toward Border 2.
3. Press Border 1-2 to Border 3, right sides together and keeping Border 1-2 on top. Align raw edges and sew down the length using the edge of the just-sewn seam allowance as your guide. Sew slowly and straight. This seam creates the narrow $^{1}/_{4}"$ border.
4. Press stitches, then press seam allowance toward Border 3.
5. Repeat 1 through 4 three times.

Sew the four borders to the quilt top, starting and stopping $^{1}/_{4}"$ from corners. Refer to page 34 for Mitering Corners by Hand.

The quilt top is complete and ready for marking quilting lines, basting, quilting, and binding. Use 2" wide straight grain double fold binding. Apply with $^{1}/_{4}"$ seam allowance.

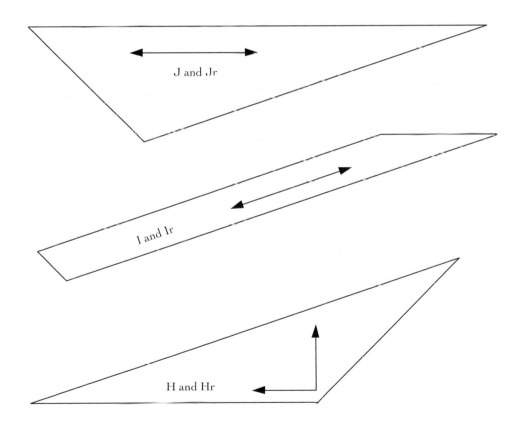

Add $^{1}/_{4}"$ seam allowance to all sides of each shape. Arrow indicates grain line.

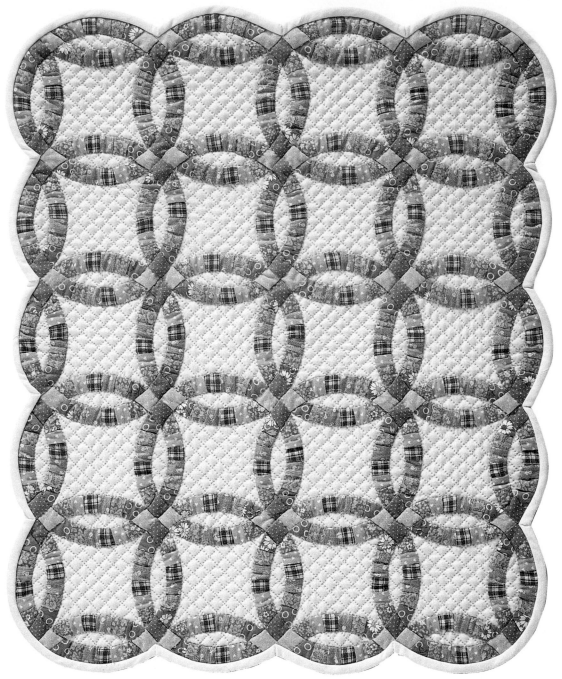

Pieced Double Wedding Ring, 18" x 22". Machine Pieced and Hand Quilted by Author.

PIECED DOUBLE WEDDING RING

The Double Wedding Ring has always been a favorite pattern of mine. It is romantic, traditional and, in my mind's eye, usually 1930ish, which leads to my fabric choices. I've made several bed size Double Wedding Ring quilts, and have framed a few small ones. I really wanted to do a smaller, pieced one and draft it myself. The book *Quilts Galore!* by Diana McClun and

Laura Nownes gives excellent instructions for drafting any size Double Wedding Ring.

This quilt is easily sewn if you follow each step in order. It requires a significant amount of preparation time before you sew. Be patient and accurate as you make the templates, mark the fabric, and do the cutting.

- Finished Quilt Size: 18" x 22"
- Ring Size: 6¹/₈"
- Techniques Used: Templates, Y-seams

Fabric Requirements:
- Arcs: ¹/₄ yard each of six different fabrics
- Posts: ¹/₄ yard each of two different fabrics
- Background: 1 yard
- Binding: Approximately 120" of 2" wide bias, double fold
- Backing: 22" x 26"
- Batting: 22" x 26"

Recommendations:
1. Lay out snips of Fabrics 1–6 (arc) in order for reference.
2. When instructed to sew dot to dot, it is helpful to sew very close to the dot without ever sewing into it. The dots should remain obvious and apparent.

Not sewing into the dot will give you smooth, flat results. Refer to Y-seam construction on page 102 in the *Santa Fe* project.

3. Layer, mark, and cut fabric exactly as described. A sandpaper board is helpful for stabilizing fabric when tracing around templates.
4. Finger-press and manipulate seams with hands and fingers before using the iron.
5. Press often and carefully with a hot dry iron, taking care not to scorch or stretch the fabric.
6. Trim seams to alleviate bulk in rings (Fabrics 1–8). When sewing Shape D and Shape E in place, you will be sewing dot to dot, which means the seams will remain free and you can wait to trim these seams until the end if you choose.
7. Most important—make a test arc before marking and cutting all the fabric.

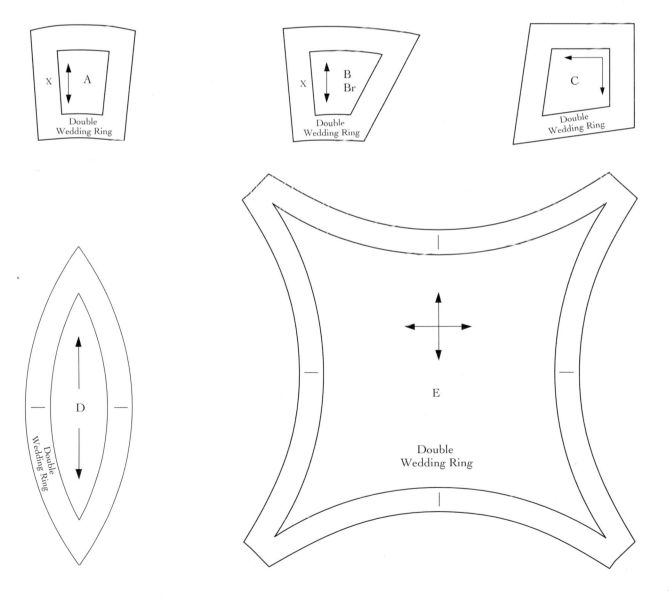

Templates

1. Make accurate templates. Transfer all information to the plastic template material. Punch holes at intersections. Refer to Templates on page 25.
2. Align template shapes as if you were sewing them together. The holes, edges, and sewing lines should match up.
3. When marking fabric, be sure the template is face down on the wrong side of the fabric. Align grain arrows with the straight grain of the fabric. Make dots on the wrong side of all fabric shapes except Shape A. The "x" shows what edges to sew.
4. Be sure you are sewing with the same seam allowance that is reflected on your templates.

Shape A

Use Fabrics 2–5. You do not need to mark dots on any of the Shape A's. Refer to your snips of fabric often to be sure the correct fabric corresponds with the correct number.

1. Trace Shape A 98 times face down on the wrong side of Fabric 3. Press Fabric 3 to 2, right sides together on grain. Pin as needed and cut out shapes, keeping them in pairs, positioning and stacking them all the same way. Set aside in box or baggie.

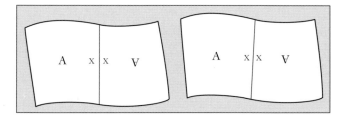

2. Trace Shape A 98 times face down on the wrong side of Fabric 5. Repeat Step 1 using Fabrics 5 and 4.

Shape B

The end piece of the arc is not symmetrical and requires special attention when sewing. The correct edges must be sewn or the arc will be misshaped.

Trace Shape B 98 times face down on the wrong side of Fabric 6 and mark dots. Press Fabric 6 to 1, right sides together on grain. Pin as needed and cut out B shapes. Separate into two piles, mark dots on wrong side of Fabric 1 shapes, set aside in box or baggie. You now have all the arc pieces cut (Fabrics 1–6).

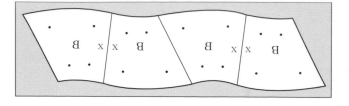

Shape C

This is the post. Trace Shape C 50 times face down on the wrong side of Fabric 7 and mark the dots. Press to Fabric 8, right sides together on grain. Pin as needed and cut out C Shapes. Separate, mark the dots on the wrong side of Fabric 8 shapes, and set aside in box or baggie. You will have two extra pieces of Fabric 8. You now have all the post pieces cut.

Shape D

Cut 49 from background fabric.

Shape E

Cut 20 from background fabric.

Arc Assembly

1. Sew all pairs of Fabrics 2–3 and 4–5 together, being sure you are sewing the correct edges. Sew with an accurate and straight $1/4"$ seam allowance in a chain piecing manner. Do not press.
2. Now join the two pairs together, sewing the correct edges. Refer to the snips of fabric to maintain the correct order. When all pairs are sewn, carefully press all seams toward Fabric 2. You should be able to take the Shape A template and place it right side up on the right side of the four-fabric arc unit and align the seams with the lines on the template.

3. Now add the correct Shape B onto each end of the arc unit. Be sure you have dots on all B shapes. Sew the correct edges, referring to the snips of fabric. You should have 98 arc units of Fabrics 1 through 6. Press all seams toward Fabric 1. If unit is correct and accurate, trim the seams.

4. Sew a Shape C post Fabric 7 to each end of 25 arcs, pinning at dots to align fabric, sewing edge to edge.

Press

5. Sew a Shape C post Fabric 8 to each end of 24 arcs, pinning at dots to align fabric, sewing edge to edge.

Press

6. You should have 49 unposted arcs left. Sew a Shape D to each of the 49 unposted arcs. With Shape D on top, match and pin center dot to center seam of arc and end dots to dots on shape B. Sew from dot to dot and backstitch. This is a soft curve, so the two edges will easily rest on each other between the three pins. Keep the arc smooth underneath. The seam allowances should be coming toward you. Finger-press seam allowance toward arc, press well with the iron.

7. Sew a posted arc to the other side of each Shape D, aligning and pinning centers and ends as described above, keeping Shape D on top while sewing.

8. Stitch the post Shape C edge and the Shape B edge together, pinning at the dots. Sew from the edge to the dot and backstitch. Press all seams in the same direction and away from the melon (Shape D). You should have 25 melon/arc units with Fabric 7 on them and 24 melon/arc units with Fabric 8 on them, for a total of 49 melon/arc units.

Quilt Assembly

1. Lay out all the melon/arc units with the Shape E backgrounds to form the quilt. Notice that all melon/arc units with Fabric 7 are positioned vertically and the melon/arc units with Fabric 8 are positioned horizontally.

2. Referring to the illustration, sew melon/arc units to Shape E, right sides together matching and pinning the center dot of E to the center seam of the arc and the end dots of E to the post intersection. Sew with Shape E on top, from dot to dot, and backstitch. Finger-press to arc, then press with an iron, carefully.

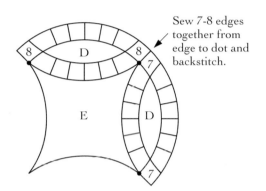

Sew 7-8 edges together from edge to dot and backstitch.

3. Add additional melon/arc units to Shape E per diagram on next page to form Rows 1 through 5. Make one X melon/arc unit, seven Y melon/arc units, and twelve Z melon arc units.

4. Sew rows, always stopping at the dot and backstitching at the post intersections.

5. Carefully press seam allowance toward arc. Quilt top is complete.

Finishing

1. Mark any quilting lines, if appropriate.

2. Layer and baste quilt top, batting, and backing. Quilt and bind.

3. Bias binding is necessary to bind the curved edges of this quilt. Apply the bias binding with a $1/4$" seam allowance and allow plenty of binding as you go around the curves. Sew to the inside point, stopping at the $1/4$" mark. Leave the needle in the fabric, lift the foot, and pivot the quilt, realigning the binding edges to the quilt edge, and continue sewing. Join the ends as described in the Binding section, page 38.

4. Sign and date the quilt on the back. Block and/or press the quilt top before displaying.

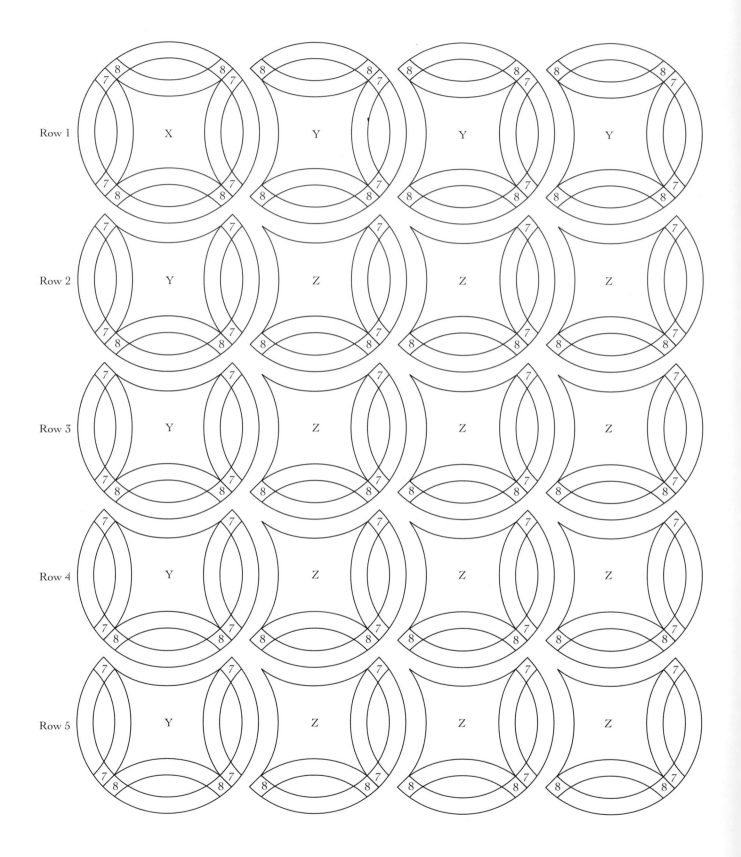

Row 1

Row 2

Row 3

Row 4

Row 5

Stepping Out, 45" Square. Machine Pieced by Author. Hand Quilted by Sheree Cowley of Simi Valley, California.

I wanted to design a contemporary feeling larger sized quilt and use small scale piecing effectively. A repeat block format of 6", 3", and 1½" Sawtooth Stars combined with a black background, the design element, and unique border treatment all contribute positively. The quilt is designed on a 1½" grid; therefore, all the

STEPPING OUT

stars interrelate.

The design element (square on point), for the most part, separates the larger stars from the smaller ones. A double sawtooth border is combined with a border print, then a final border of background value fabric is added to complete the quilt top.

- Quilt Size: 45"
  Square
- Techniques
  Used: Double
  half-square
  triangle,
  rotary cutting

Fabric Requirements:

Red and purple were my color choices, and I used lots of fabrics (30–35) to shade and expand each color. Red includes pinks to oranges; purple stretches to lavenders and blues.

Stepping Out Color Map

The variety of fabric prints and shades of color add to the interest for the viewer. See shading photo, page 18.

I chose to arrange the color to be cooler around the edges and warmer toward the center. As the quilt warms, the pieces get smaller! Generally, each star is one fabric. In a few instances, I've used more than one fabric in the star to add slight lightness or brightness and/or to move from one star to another smoothly and with interest.

Two different background fabrics were used, tone-on-tone black print and solid black cotton sateen. Notice that the inside of the design element is entirely pieced from the sateen fabric. I deliberately did this because of the way sateen shimmers when you cut it up, change the grain, and sew it back together. It quilts beautifully and offers wonderful quilting texture.

I chose the teal tone-on-tone fabric as the accent for defining the design element and to serve as the sawtooth borders. Spend a good amount of time interviewing fabric for this position; choose the fabric that makes the stars better than they are without it. Don't settle!

- Background Black: 3 yards in total
- Stars: 1³/₄ yards in total
- Accent Fabric: 1¹/₄ yard (design line and two sawtooth borders)
- Border Print: 1 yard (¹/₄ yard if cutting cross grain)
- Final Border: ¹/₂ yard (included in background yardage)
- Binding: 200" of 2" wide straight grain, double fold
- Batting: 50" square
- Backing: 50" square

Color Map

To help me visualize my large star color placement and design element area, I cut 2" squares of many different fabrics I thought might work. I then played with their placement, folding some squares into triangles to create the design. Refer to the line drawing and photo as needed. It's helpful to arrange the squares on the background color fabric you'll use. This becomes your map or guide to pair background and star fabrics for cutting and sewing. However, always remain open to change and be flexible when your quilt begins to talk.

Following your color map, cut and sew the needed units for the 6" stars; position them on the flannel wall following the diagram and filling in with the background 2" squares. Do not assemble the units and background into blocks just yet. Once they are placed, make the eight half stars. Position them following the diagram, but do not sew them together. Now place the accent fabric triangles in place to form the design element.

Note: The pieces you put up on the flannel wall include seam allowance so you will need to overlap shapes to maintain the grid.

You are now ready to interview fabric for the smaller stars, assemble them, position them referring to the diagram, and sew the interior of the quilt together.

Note: This quilt is easily redesigned and changed by moving the design line around. Experiment and play on ¹/₄" grid paper. You do not need to have a square on point. There are lots of possibilities. Sketch first for general design then fill in the grid to create the design and clarify how the quilt will be pieced together.

Fill-In Background Triangles

Seventy are needed for design element and half stars.

1. Cut three strips of background fabric 2³/₈" wide, sub-cut into thirty-five 2³/₈" squares.
2. Cut the squares in half diagonally.

One Whole 6" Star, (6½" Unfinished)
Grid Dimension: 1½"—Make 25
1. Cut four 2" squares, four 3½" x 2" rectangles, and one 3½" square of background fabric.
2. Cut twelve 2" squares of star fabric.

Half 6" Stars,
Grid Dimension: 1½"—Make 8
1. Cut one 2" square and two 3½" x 2" rectangles of background fabric; five 2⅜" Fill-In Triangles are already cut.
2. Cut four 2" squares of star fabric. Cut one 2⅜" square of star fabric, cut in half diagonally (need one triangle for each half star).

One 3" Star, (3½" Unfinished)
Grid Dimension: ¾"—Make 13
1. Cut four 1¼" squares, four 1¼" x 2" rectangles, and one 2" square of background fabric.
2. Cut twelve 1¼" squares of star fabric.

One 1½" Star, (2" Unfinished)
Grid Dimension: ⅜"— Make 14
1. Cut four ⅞" squares, four ⅞" x 1¼" rectangles, and one 1¼" square of background fabric.
2. Cut twelve ⅞" squares of star fabric.

All sizes of whole stars are made up of one Center Unit, four Star Point Units, and four corner squares. Half 6" stars consist of two Star Point Units, one square and five triangles of background fabric, and one star fabric triangle. There are 25 whole 6" stars, eight half 6" stars, thirteen 3" stars and fourteen 1½" stars. Notice that the center square of the star is always half its total size.

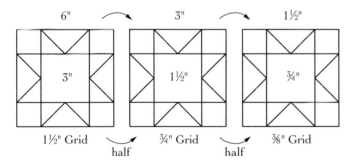

Five 3" stars (J, 2 K's, M, O) are centers of 6" stars (C, D, E, G) and have an added corner treatment. Add a 1¼" square of appropriate star fabric on each corner, sew diagonally, and flip up the corner; trim out the star fabric triangle only and press toward corner.

Two 1½" stars (P, R) are the centers of 3" stars (M, N) and have the same kind of added corner treatment as described above. The squares added to the

1½" star are ⅞" squares, sewn diagonally, trimmed, and the corner flipped up. Notice that this type of corner treatment gives the feeling that the star is in a circle (octagon) rather than a square.

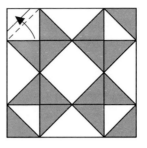

Two 1½" stars (2 Q's) are the centers of 6" stars (2 F's). Background sashing is added to bring the block up to a 3½" square. Cut two strips of background fabric 2" x 1½" and add to the sides of the star. Press stitches. Press seam toward outside edge, trim seams.

Now trim this unit to an accurate 3½" width. Measure out from the center of the block 1¾" in both directions and draw a line. Measure from line to line and if it measures 3½", cut on the drawn lines. The unit now measures 2" x 3½". Cut two strips of background fabric 3½" x 1½", sew to the top and bottom of the block, measure out from the center as illustrated; if 3½" square, trim on the drawn line. The star block is now ready to receive the large (6") star fabric 2" squares as described in Center Unit.

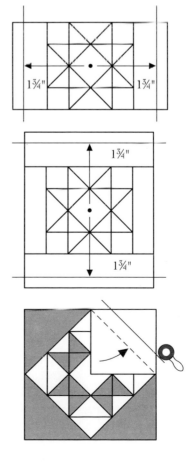

Star Point Unit

Make four star point units for each whole star, two for each half star. Refer to Double Half-Square Triangle Units, page 24, for sewing instructions. All star points use a rectangle and two squares.

Note: The suggestion to leave the rectangle in place when trimming applies to the 3" and 1¹/₂" stars only.

Center Unit

Make one Center Unit for each star desired.

Note: When doing this sew and flip technique, take care to be sure the squares do not shift and that you sew on the scrap side of the line. Press and trim properly. This unit should remain the same size as the larger square you started with.

1. Mark a diagonal line on the wrong side of four squares of star fabric.
2. Sew to the background center square as illustrated.
3. Trim away the corner triangle of the star fabric only and leave the larger background square in place for the 3" and 1¹/₂" stars. There should be no overhang of the star fabric beyond the background center square.

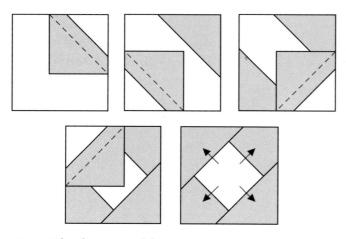

Star Block Assembly

Lay out the block and sew units and squares into rows 1–2–3, then sew rows into the completed block. Follow the appropriate pressing path for each type of star and trim seams if your work is correct and maintains the grid dimension.

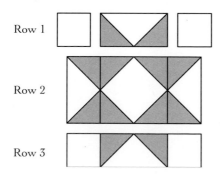

Row 1
Row 2
Row 3

Note: To form rows, you must sew the star point units to squares. This seam develops the height of the star point and must be sewn very straight and accurately to create even star points! All the stars are assembled in nearly the same way. The following are differences that occur when assembling the smaller 3" and 1¹/₂" stars.

1. Pressing path changes, some seams will be opened.
2. Trim seams to relieve and distribute bulk.
3. The background fabric rectangles and center squares remain in place.
4. The small stars will likely take longer to sew than the 6" star.

3" Stars

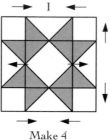

I

Make 4

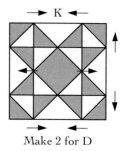

J

Make 1 for C

K

Make 2 for D

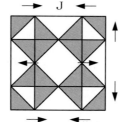

L

Make 3

M

Make 1 for E

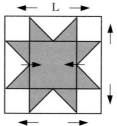
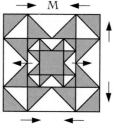

N

Make 1

O

Make 1 for G

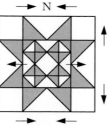
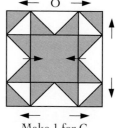

6" Stars

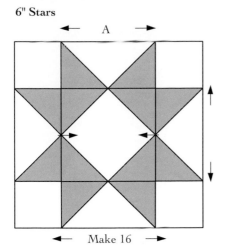

A

Make 16

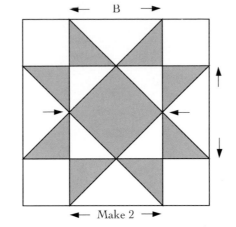

B

Make 2

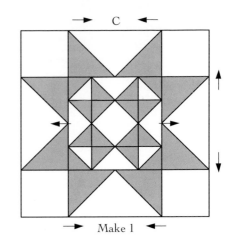

C

Make 1

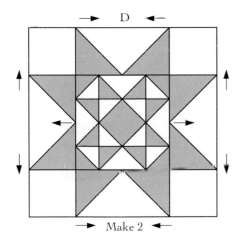

D

Make 2

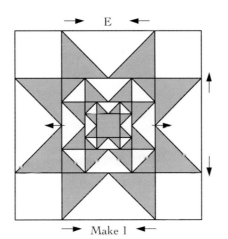

E

Make 1

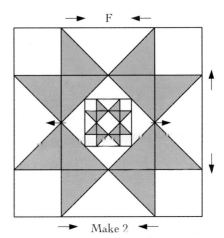

F

Make 2

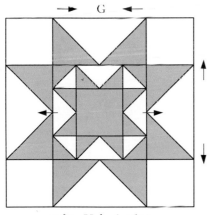

G

Make 1

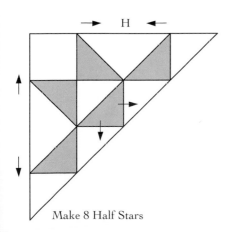

H

Make 8 Half Stars

1½" Stars

P

Make 1 for N

Q

Make 11 (2 for F)

R

Make 1 for M

S

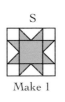

Make 1

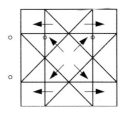

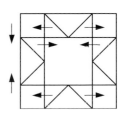

Design Element Triangles (accent fabric)

When all the whole and half large star units, background squares, and triangles are on the flannel wall (see quilt diagram, page 91), you are ready to place the 60 design element triangles.

Cut two $2^3/_8$" wide strips of accent fabric and sub-cut into twenty-eight $2^3/_8$" squares. Cut the squares in half diagonally. Cut two $2^3/_8$" squares of the chosen Half 6" Star fabric. Cut the squares in half diagonally. Place all sixty triangles on the flannel wall, referring to the diagram. The star fabric triangles extend the Half 6" Stars into the design element.

Inside the Design Element

Now you can cut smaller squares ($1^1/_4$" and $^7/_8$") from the chosen small star fabrics; place them inside the design element, following the diagram and grid,

creating a color map as you did for 6" stars to interview color inside the design element. Remember, smaller pieces need more intense color. There is also one 6" star inside the design element as well.

Sew all the small stars (3" and $1^1/_2$") into blocks and place on the flannel inside and out of design element. Referring to diagram, make the appropriate units and background to form the one 6" (E) star inside as well. Now cut two 2" wide strips of background fabric and sub-cut into twenty-eight 2" squares. Fill in with the background squares and previously cut triangles until the interior of the design element is formed and complete. Refer to diagram below.

Carefully evaluate and compare the fabric grid you have created to the paper grid. Join the loose triangles into appropriate squares, pressing seams to accent fabric. Assemble the 24 whole star blocks on the

Star Placement Diagram

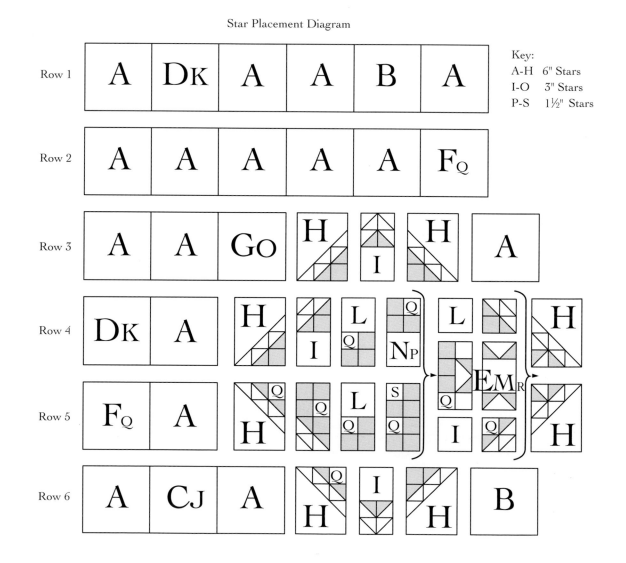

Key:
A-H 6" Stars
I-O 3" Stars
P-S 1½" Stars

outside of the design element and begin to develop Rows 1 through 6. Join rows, matching points and intersections carefully, maintaining the grid dimension. Press well. Notice that Rows 4 and 5 are joined differently.

Note: Because this quilt is designed on a grid of $1\frac{1}{2}$" squares, the dimensions of the quilt should now be $36\frac{1}{2}$" square and the pieced border is developed based on the same grid dimension.

Sawtooth Borders

The project quilt uses a sawtooth border in two different sizes. The sawteeth are made by pairing a background triangle to an accent triangle and sewing them into a square.

Large Sawtooth Border:
Grid Dimension: $1\frac{1}{2}$", Make 56 Units

Cut two $2\frac{3}{8}$" strips each of the background and accent fabric. Sub-cut into twenty-eight $2\frac{3}{8}$" squares and cut in half diagonally. You should have 56 triangles of each fabric.

Small Sawtooth Border:
Grid Dimension: $\frac{3}{4}$", Make 124 Units

Cut three $1\frac{5}{8}$" strips each of the background and accent fabric. Sub-cut into 62 squares and cut in half diagonally. You should have 124 triangles of each fabric.

1. Half-Square Triangle Units: Pair the background and accent triangles, right sides together, and sew along the bias edges with an accurate $\frac{1}{4}$" seam allowance. Press the large unit seam allowance toward the accent fabric; the small unit seam allowance should be pressed opened and trimmed. Don't forget to set the seam before final pressing. This is quite important to do when joining triangles to form squares. Trim the ears and measure to be sure each large sawtooth unit measures 2" square and the small sawtooth unit measures $1\frac{1}{4}$" square.

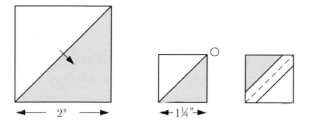

2. Additional background pieces are needed to join the sawtooth border to the border print, to change the direction of the sawteeth, and to develop the corner squares. From background fabric cut: eight

$1\frac{1}{4}$" x 2" rectangles, two $2\frac{3}{4}$" squares (draw a diagonal line on the wrong side of these squares), nine $1\frac{1}{4}$" squares, and two 2" squares.

3. Border Print: Cut two strips 36" x $2\frac{3}{4}$" ($2\frac{1}{4}$" finished). One end of each strip should be cut at the same place in the border print. This is the end to be joined to the sawteeth, not the mitered end.

4. Corner Unit: Make three corner units as illustrated using the $1\frac{1}{4}$" sawtooth units, $1\frac{1}{4}$" background squares and $1\frac{1}{4}$" x 2" rectangles. Set aside.

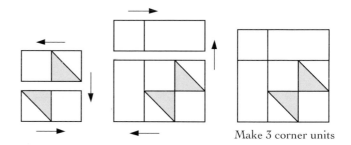

Make 3 corner units

Border A Assembly

1. Sew 23 large sawtooth units and one background square together, maintaining $1\frac{1}{2}$" grid dimension. Press seams toward background triangles.

2. Sew 48 small sawtooth units together, taking care to maintain a $\frac{3}{4}$" grid dimension. Press seams open and trim.

3. Sew large sawtooth border unit to small sawtooth border unit, matching and pinning intersections and seams accurately. Press stitches, then press seam allowance toward small sawtooth border unit, carefully finger-pressing ahead of the iron. Because borders with so many seams are easily distorted, handle and press carefully.

Border B Assembly

1. Border B combines sawtooth units and a border print. Sew five large sawtooth units together maintaining a $1\frac{1}{2}$" grid dimension and press seam toward background triangles. Add a background rectangle and press seam toward background triangle.

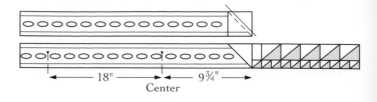

2. Sew eleven small sawtooth units together, maintain $3/4$" grid dimension. Press the seams open and trim.

3. Sew large and small sawtooth borders together, matching and pinning seams and intersections, press stitches, press seam toward small sawtooth border unit, pressing carefully as described in Step 3 of Border A Assembly.

4. Sew background square to correct end of border print, right sides together and position diagonal line correctly. Sew on the drawn line, flip corner up to meet the other, trim and press toward background. Now sew border print to sawteeth and press seam toward border print.

Border C Assembly

Border C also joins sawtooth units with a border print. Assemble as described in Border B above. Add a corner unit at correct end, press seam toward corner unit.

Border D Assembly

1. Sew 23 large sawtooth units and one background square together, maintaining $1\frac{1}{2}$" grid dimension. Press seams toward background triangles.

2. Sew 48 small sawtooth units together, maintaining $3/4$" grid dimension. Press seams open and trim.

3. Sew large and small sawtooth border units together, matching and pinning seams, press stitches, then press seam toward small sawteeth.

4. Add a corner unit to each end of Border D, press seam allowance toward corner units. Before adding the borders to the quilt top, you must mark the center and ends of Borders B and C. To find the center, measure $9\frac{3}{4}$" from the joining point of the border print and the sawteeth and place a pin. To find the ends, measure out from the center pin 18" and place a pin. This pin is where you will stop sewing and backstitch when adding Borders B and C to the quilt. This allows enough fabric so the corner can be mitered.

Sewing the Borders to the Quilt Top

1. Referring to illustration, add Border A to the left side of the quilt top, matching and pinning centers and ends of border and quilt top. Add additional pins as needed. Sew with Border A on top, press stitches, then press seam toward quilt top.

2. Add Border B to right side of quilt, matching and pinning centers and ends of border to quilt. The pin at the end mark of the border print gets matched to the corner of the quilt, $1/4$" in from the edge. When sewing, the border will be on the bottom, the quilt on the top, sew from edge to $1/4$" mark and backstitch. Press stitches and then press seam toward quilt top.

3. Add Border C to quilt top, matching and pinning centers and ends of border to quilt. The pin at the end mark of the border print gets matched to the corner of the quilt, $1/4$" in from the edge. When sewing, the border will be on the top. Press stitches and then press seam toward quilt top.

4. Now miter the B-C corner. Refer to Mitering Corners by Hand on page 34.

5. Sew Border D to quilt bottom, matching and pinning centers and ends of border to quilt, as well as intersections and seams. Sew with the border on the top, press stitches, then press seam to quilt top.

Final Border

1. Press the quilt top well and carefully, manipulating and maintaining squareness. There are a lot of seams in this quilt, so the opportunities for stretching are great; take care when handling.

2. Measure the quilt down and across the center. Because the quilt is square and based on $1\frac{1}{2}$" grid, mathematically the quilt should measure 41" square. It is very likely, however, that the quilt measures close but not exactly because of all the seaming. The opportunity for discrepancy is also great. What you want is a measurement that is the same for all four borders. If the vertical and horizontal measurements are different but close, average.

3. Cut four final border strips all the same length and 3" wide.

4. Create four corner four-patch blocks, using two background fabrics as illustrated.

5. Cut one $1^3/_4$" x 40" strip of two fabrics. Pair them, right sides together, and sew down the length with a $^1/_4$" seam allowance. Press stitches, then press seam toward one of the strips.

6. Cut eight $1^3/_4$" segments. Sew two $1^3/_4$" segments, match outside edges and inner seam. Press stitches, then press the seam as indicated. This four-patch unit should measure 3" square.

7. Sew borders and corner four-patch squares to quilt using diagram as your guide. Press stitches, then press seam toward outside edge of the quilt.

Quilt top is complete and ready to baste, quilt, and bind. Apply binding with $^1/_4$" seam allowance.

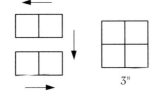

3"

Quilt Diagram

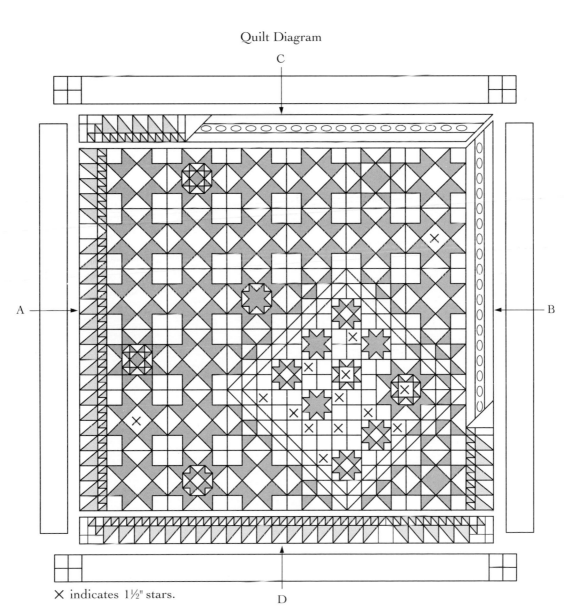

C

A

B

D

✗ indicates $1^1/_2$" stars.

Shadow Baskets, 28 1/2" Square. Pieced and Quilted by Author.

SHADOW BASKETS

I wanted to do a very pretty, traditional quilt that would combine several different techniques and elements.

Baskets, in two sizes, set on point and separated by sashing and posts reflect that theme. The sawtooth border echoes the basket triangles. The swag adds softness, romance, and charm, while the piping adds the unexpected detail.

Take your time, enjoy the journey.

- Quilt Size: 28½" square
- Small Basket: 1⅞" finished,
  Grid dimension: ⅜"
- Large Basket: 3⅛" finished,
  Grid dimension: ⅝"
- Techniques Used: Oversized half-square triangle, half-square triangle—bias strip method, templates, appliqué, strip piecing, piping, bias binding
- Tools: Quilters GluTube®, freezer paper, Bias Square®, Hot Tape™

Fabric Requirements:

The photo on page 18 displays all the fabrics used in this quilt. I pulled five colors from the floral palette fabric: purple, pink, green, brown, and blue. To stretch and expand each color, I chose several different prints and values of each, and decided to accentuate the pink and green, while the other colors harmonized with the theme.

Note that the brightest colors in the project quilt are in the smallest pieces. The larger prints (relatively speaking) are in the larger shapes, which take maximum advantage of the fabric.

- Baskets: 16" total of bias length for each small basket and large basket. I work with ¼-yard pieces of fabric and cut multiple strips to gain the 16" length needed.
- Background or light area: 1¾ yards total. The project quilt uses four different light fabrics:
  Basket Background light fabric: ½ yard
  Sashing light fabric: ¼ yard
  Side Triangle and Corner light fabric: ¼ yard
  Sawtooth and Swag light fabric: ¾ yard
  Sawtooth Border medium fabric: ¼ yard
- Accent Fabric (swags, sashing, four-patches, piping): ½ yard
- Border 1: ⅛ yard
- Border 2: ⅓ yard
- Cording for piping: 4 yards ⅛" wide
- Bias Binding: 144" of 2¼" wide bias grain, double fold
- Backing: 32" square
- Batting: 32" square

One Small Basket:
(1⅞" Finished, 2⅜" Unfinished)
Grid Dimension: ⅜"—Make 13

1. Shape A: Cut one 2" square of light fabric (I used the same fabric for all the baskets). Cut one 2" square of basket fabric. Use larger prints to show some visual texture.
2. Shape B: Cut 1½" wide bias strips of basket and background fabric. You need a total of 16" in length for each basket (generous). You will need to cut two strips if you are using ¼-yard pieces of fabric. Shape B will be made in pairs using the bias strip method, which will create accurate, pressed, half-square triangle units with straight grain on the outside edges.
3. Shape C: Cut two ⅞" x 1⅝" rectangles from background fabric.
4. Shape D: Cut one ⅞" square from background.
5. AA Unit: Draw a diagonal line on the wrong side of the lightest A square. Pair both A squares, right sides together, and sew on the drawn line. Open to show two triangles, press seam toward basket fabric and trim seam to a generous ⅛". This AA unit is oversized and must now be trimmed to an exact 1⅝" square using the Bias Square and keeping the 45° angle line on the Bias Square positioned on the seam to ensure an equal split diagonally. Refer to Oversized Half-Square Triangle Units, page 24.
6. BB Unit: Refer to Half-Square Triangle Units— Bias Strip Method on page 22 for sewing, pressing and cutting instructions. From the sewn bias strips, develop a 45° angle, cut nine ⅞" slices, and sub-cut those into ⅞" squares.
7. Referring to the block diagram, lay out the block and evaluate carefully to be sure all the triangles are positioned correctly. It's easy to get the B's turned wrong.
8. Following the illustration, sew the block. Arrows and circles indicate pressing directions. Trim all seams if grid dimension is maintained. Press well. The small basket block should measure 2⅜" square as you hold it in your hand. Make 12 more small baskets.

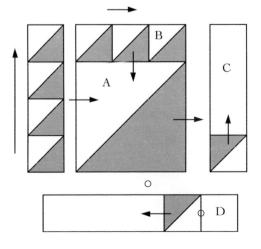

One Large Basket:
(3$\frac{1}{8}$" Finished, 3$\frac{5}{8}$" Unfinished)

Grid Dimension: $\frac{5}{8}$"—Make 13

1. Shape E: Cut 1$\frac{1}{2}$" wide bias strips of basket and background fabric. You need a total of 16" in length for each basket (generous). You will need to cut two strips if you are using $\frac{1}{4}$-yard pieces.
2. Shape F: Cut two 1$\frac{1}{8}$" x 2$\frac{3}{8}$" rectangles from background fabric.
3. Shape G: Cut one 1$\frac{1}{8}$" square from background fabric.
4. EE Unit: Refer to Half-Square Triangle—Bias Strip Method, page 22, for sewing, pressing, and cutting instructions. Cut nine 1$\frac{1}{8}$" slices from the bias strip and sub-cut into nine 1$\frac{1}{8}$" squares.
5. Lay out the E, F, and G shapes around the small basket and sew as diagramed. Arrows indicate pressing. All seams should be trimmed if grid dimension is maintained. Completed block should measure 3$\frac{5}{8}$" square as you hold it in your hand. Make 12 more large baskets.

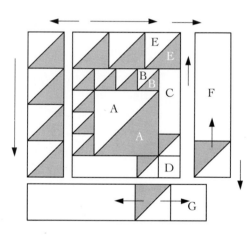

Sashing
The sashing is divided into three areas. The two outside strips are light and make the basket blocks float and appear less crowded, while the center strip of accent fabric frames and organizes the blocks.

1. Cut eight $\frac{7}{8}$" x 40" strips of light sashing fabric ($\frac{3}{8}$" finished). Cut four $\frac{3}{4}$" x 40" strips of accent fabric ($\frac{1}{4}$" finished).
2. Sew two sashing and one accent fabric strips together. Press stitches, then press seam toward accent fabric. The seam allowances must be trimmed carefully so that the two edges meet underneath the accent fabric and do not overlap. The three-strip unit should measure 1$\frac{1}{2}$" from edge to edge. Repeat three more times.
3. Matching ruler lines on seam lines, cut thirty-six 3$\frac{5}{8}$" rectangles.

4. On a flannel board lay out the baskets and sashing, using the diagram as a guide. Move the baskets around to position them in a pleasing manner, balancing the color.

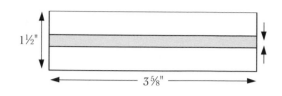

Posts
Make 12 four-patches. Choose two fabrics that reinforce your color scheme.

1. Cut one 1" x 40" straight strip from each fabric. Pair the two strips right sides together and press. Sew down the length with an accurate $\frac{1}{4}$" seam allowance, press stitches, press seam toward one side. Strip set should measure 1$\frac{1}{2}$" from edge to edge. Trim seam.
2. Develop a straight edge on one end and cut twenty-four 1" segments.
3. Arrange two segments into a four-patch as illustrated, matching and pinning center intersection and outside edges. Sew with an accurate $\frac{1}{4}$" seam allowance.
4. Press stitches, open to a square, press seam allowance toward one side. The four-patch should measure 1$\frac{1}{2}$" square, as you hold it in your hand. Trim the seam. Repeat for the remaining 11 posts. Place posts on flannel board using quilt photo as guide.

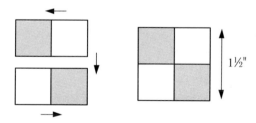

Corner Turn Block
Make 12 of these blocks, which are an extension of the sashing and help the eye turn the corner and complete the design element.

1. Cut one $\frac{7}{8}$" x 20" strip of sashing fabric, sub-cut into twelve 1$\frac{1}{2}$" segments.
2. Cut one $\frac{7}{8}$" x 20" strip of sashing fabric. Cut one 1$\frac{1}{8}$" x 20" strip of accent fabric. Pair these two strips, right sides together, press, then sew down the length with an accurate $\frac{1}{4}$" seam allowance. Press stitches. Press seam toward sashing fabric. Strip unit should measure 1$\frac{1}{2}$" from edge to edge. Sub-cut twelve $\frac{3}{4}$" segments.

3. Cut one $^7/_8$" x 40" strip of sashing fabric, cut in half. Cut one $^3/_4$" x 20" strip of accent fabric. Sew the three strips together, press stitches, and then press seams toward accent fabric and trim so both seam allowances meet and lay underneath the accent fabric as was done for the sashing. The three-strip unit should measure $1^1/_2$" from edge to edge. Sub-cut into twelve $^7/_8$" segments.

4. Arrange one segment from each strip unit and sew together, referring to illustration. Carefully match and pin seams so that the accent fabric travels around the corners smoothly. Press following the arrows. The block should measure $1^1/_2$" square; trim seams. Repeat 11 more times.

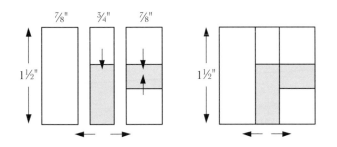

Note: You will have seam intersections where the seam allowances will be going the same direction. It is helpful, as you are sewing and approach this intersection, to lift the presser foot slightly and reposition the work so that both layers go under the needle evenly rather than the top layer being pushed ahead, creating a mismatched intersection.

5. Place corner turn blocks on flannel board using quilt photo as guide.

Side Triangles and Corners

This is the area where the value remains light, but the visual texture of the fabric is larger, creating interest. The side triangles and corners are each fragmented into three areas, similar to the sashing. Strips of light and accent fabric are joined together and then a template is placed on the strip unit, matching lines on template with seams. Make templates for Shape H and I, transferring all placement lines. Add $^1/_4$" seam allowance to all sides.

Shape H—Side Triangle: Make 8

1. Cut two 3" x 40" strips from light fabric. Cut one $^3/_4$" x 40" strip from accent fabric.

2. Join strips, press all seams in one direction.

3. Place Shape H template face down on the wrong side of the strip unit, matching lines on the template with stitching lines. If both lines are not in alignment, match the same line consistently. Turn template to minimize waste. Trace and cut eight times. Place on flannel board using diagram as guide.

Add $^1/_4$" seam allowance to all sides.

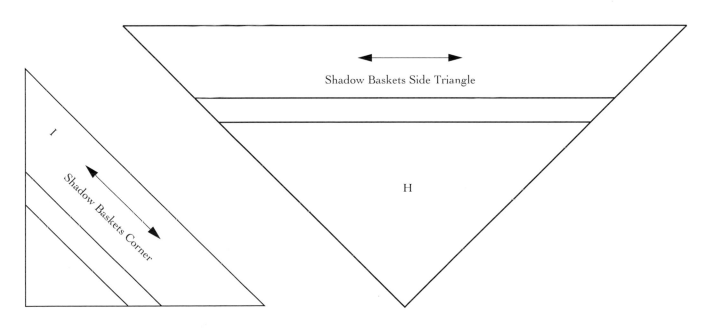

Shadow Baskets Side Triangle

Shadow Baskets Corner

I

H

Shape I—Corner: Make 8

1. Cut two $1\frac{1}{2}$" x 40" strips from light fabric. Cut one $\frac{3}{4}$" x 40" strip from accent fabric.
2. Sew strips as described in Shape H.
3. Place Template I face down on the wrong side of the strip unit, matching lines and seams consistently. Trace and cut eight times.
4. Place two shape I's together four times. Sew and match seam lines to create a smooth corner turn. Open the seam; place on the flannel board using diagram as guide.

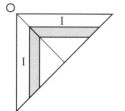

Quilt Assembly

Sew sashing, blocks, and side triangles together and sashing, posts, and corner turn blocks together to create Rows 1 through 5. Notice that the quilt is assembled in diagonal rows. Press carefully, paying close attention to pressing direction. Match all post intersections.

Sawtooth Border

I chose one light fabric and one medium green for all the sawteeth to balance the pink of the sashing color and to reinforce the pink and green theme. Thirty-eight sawteeth are needed for each side, for a total of 152. The direction of the border changes in the middle of each side. The sawteeth are $\frac{1}{2}$" finished (grid dimension) and are made using the bias strip method. Refer to Half-Square Triangle Units — Bias Strip Method on page 22 for details on how to sew, press,

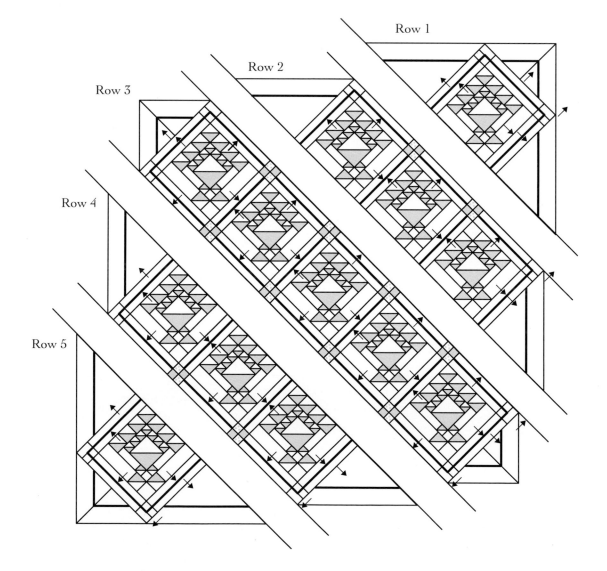

and trim strips. When you make sawtooth borders, there are many seams and the opportunity for stretching is increased.

As you join the sawteeth, stay attentive to maintaining grid dimension and continue to measure (for example, if four sawteeth are sewn together, they should measure:

$$1/2" + 1/2" + 1/2" + 1/2" \text{ (four grids) } = 2"$$
$$+ 1/2" \text{ seam allowance } = 2\,1/2"$$

1. Cut four 1" squares of light fabric for the four corners.
2. Pair $1/4$ yard of the medium sawtooth fabric with $1/4$ yard of the light fabric, right sides together, press well, develop a 45° angle on one end, and cut ten $1\,1/2"$ bias strips. Remove the medium fabric and continue to cut ten more bias strips of light fabric.
3. Sew the paired medium and light strips down the length, press stitches, open seam with your hands carefully, then press and trim. Repeat for the nine remaining pairs.
4. Add the remaining ten light strips to the opposite side of the medium fabric, sew, press, and trim as described in Step 3.
5. Develop a 45° angle on the three-strip units and cut seventy-six 1" slices, keeping the angle accurate by aligning the 45° angle line on the ruler with one of the seams; the 1" line should be on the edge of your fabric.
6. From each 1" slice, cut two 1" squares, to equal 152. Always align the 45° angle line of the ruler on the seam line.

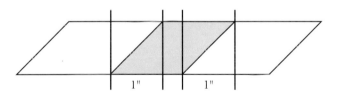

7. Sew 19 sawteeth in one direction and 19 sawteeth in the opposite direction, four times. Join two sets of 19 sawteeth, four times, to create the four borders.

Note: Sew very straight and accurately, maintaining the $1/2"$ grid dimension. Sew singles into pairs, then pairs into foursomes, etc. Work with 19 at a time and be sure you are sewing the correct edges. Press seams in one direction; trim.

8. Sew two borders to the sides of the quilt, sawtooth border on top. Press seam toward quilt.
9. Add two squares to each end of two remaining sawtooth borders, press toward square.

10. Sew remaining sawtooth borders to quilt top and bottom. Sew with borders on top. Press stitches, press seam toward quilt. Do adequate pinning, first at centers and ends, then evenly distribute the border along the quilt edge. Your quilt top should be $20\,1/2"$ square after the sawtooth borders are applied.

Sides
Make 2

Top/Bottom
Make 2

Swag Border

1. Cut four $2\,1/2"$ x 20" strips and four $2\,1/2"$ squares of light fabric. The project quilt uses the same light fabric as the sawtooth border.
2. Press each border strip in half and place a pin at the fold to identify the center. Place a pin at the centers of all four sides of the quilt top.
3. Sew the two side borders to the quilt top right sides together, matching center and corner pins of borders and quilt top. Use additional pins as needed to create smooth sewing. Press the stitches, then press seams toward outside edge of quilt top.
4. Sew two squares to each end of the remaining two border strips and press away from the corner. Sew to top and bottom of quilt, matching corner intersections and centers. Pin to create smooth sewing. Press stitches, then press toward outside edge of quilt.

Note: The swags and corners will be cut out and appliquéd to the quilt top after the final mitered borders are sewn on and the quilt top is complete.

Mitered Borders

The narrow inner border is a medium green in the project quilt, much like the sawtooth border fabric, followed by the final border of the original palette fabric. Because I knew I would quilt heavily in this project, I oversized the width of the final border, which gave me the opportunity to square up before binding. I wanted the border to finish 2", so I cut 3" wide strips.

1. Cut four $3/4"$ x 35" strips from the inner border fabric and four 3" x 35" strips from the final border fabric.
2. Sew one inner border strip and one final border strip, right sides together with narrow border on top, down the length. Press stitches, finger-press seam toward outside edge, and press with iron. Repeat three more times.

3. Refer to Mitering Corners by Hand on page 34 after sewing the borders to the quilt top, starting and stopping $^1/_4$" from corners.

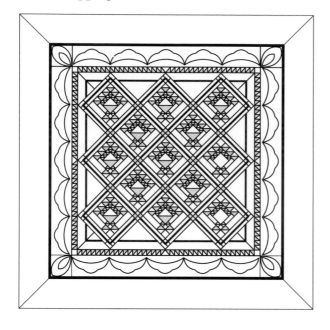

Swags and Corners

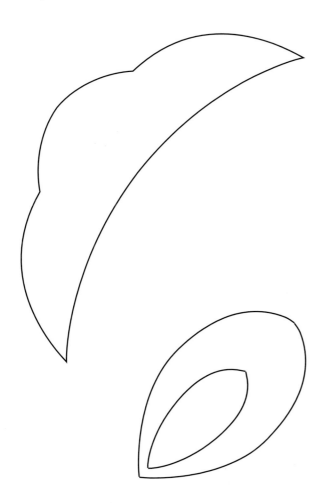

The swag border adds a gentle softness, as it continues the pretty, feminine feeling and complements the basket design.

1. Trace and cut 20 swag shapes and four corner shapes from freezer paper.
2. Press freezer paper shapes, shiny side down, to wrong side of appropriate fabric, leaving room between the shapes for seam allowance.
3. Using the Quilters GluTube®, apply glue to both fabric and paper about $^3/_{16}$" on each.
4. Let the glue dry.

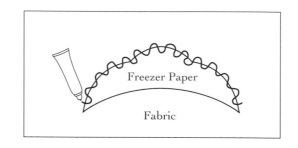

5. Cut out one shape at a time, allowing for $^3/_{16}$" seam allowance from the paper edge.
6. Bring the fabric over the paper edge smoothly, clipping at inside points when you get there. Repeat for all the swag and corner shapes.

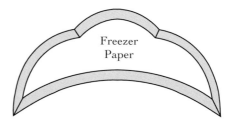

7. Once all the swags and corners are prepared, place two corners and five swags on one side and evaluate for fit and placement. Hold the shapes in place with Hot Tape™, which allows you to iron on it and remove it without leaving a residue, and it can be reused. Pinning or thread basting are also options for holding the shapes in place while appliquéing.
8. Hand appliqué the shapes in place with well-matched thread and tiny stitches. Appliqué the inside curve of the five swags and corners first, then do the outside curve. Repeat for the remaining three sides and two corners.
9. Turn the quilt over and cut out the background fabric to within $^3/_{16}$" from the appliqué stitches. Release and remove the paper by gently tugging with hands or tweezers. Always hold the stitches

between your fingers as you tug at the paper so as not to distress the fabric. If a little paper gets left in the sharp points, it's okay.

10. Place the quilt top on a soft towel, face down, and steam press the appliqué area gently, if necessary. Quilt top is now complete.

Quilting

When I was making this quilt I could already see how I wanted to quilt. I like the relief (texture) quilting creates in very straight lines or grids, as in the side triangles and corners, and I also wanted to reinforce the curved shapes of the swags by echo quilting. The final border is also quilted, but the print prevents the eye from seeing the design clearly. The interior of the quilt is all seam or "in-the-ditch" quilted by machine, which helps to keep the quilt square and also saved time. The quilting stitches that you can see are done by hand; the quilting around the baskets, sashing, and borders is all done by machine.

Binding

1. Refer to Preparing the Quilt for Binding on page 37 and square up the corners and sides. Develop and mark a line around the quilt 2¼" from the last seam.

2. Round each corner by using a drinking glass or similar tool, align it with the two sides, and draw the curve. Repeat for all four corners. This line will be your guide when applying the piping and binding. Do not cut until the binding is sewn on and ends are joined.

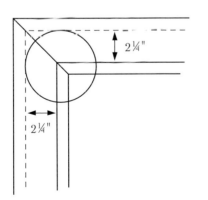

3. Prepare 144" of continuous bias piping. See Piping on page 39.

4. Prepare 144" x 2¼" of bias double fold binding.

5. Using a zipper foot, sew piping to folded binding with piping on top, keeping all raw edges together and sewing on top of the existing piping stitches. The stitch length can be lengthened for this process. Sew very precisely and slowly.

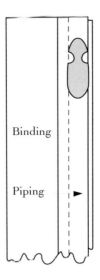

6. Continue to use the zipper foot and sew the piping/binding to the quilt top (binding on top with the piping closest to the quilt top), leaving about a 2" tail before you begin stitching. Align all the raw edges to the drawn line on the quilt top. Sew just inside the visible stitches, toward the piping. Sew slowly and carefully, being generous with the piping/binding when going around the corners. Clip the piping/binding only, not the quilt, when rounding corners to help the corners lay flat. Sew all the way around the quilt to within about four inches of the starting stitches and remove from the machine.

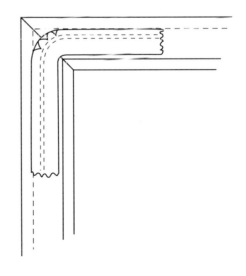

7. The ends of the binding/piping will be joined separately, which means you will release stitches, arrange the two, and then sew to the quilt top as one again. Trim ending tail so it overlaps beginning tail by 1". On the beginning and ending tails, release about 1½" of binding from the piping.

8. Pin binding back and away from both piping ends.
9. Release about 1½" of stitching from the ending piping tail only, and cut 1" of the cording off. Turn the raw edge under ¼" and finger-press.
10. Insert beginning piping tail into the ending tail; align all raw edges. Pin piping in place with one pin parallel to the edge.

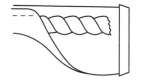

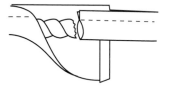

11. Fold raw edge of binding ending tail under about ¼" and finger-press. Lay beginning tail inside the ending tail and trim so that raw edges are covered but you are not creating unnecessary bulk.

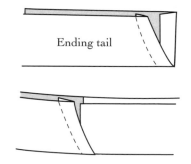

Ending tail

12. Lay binding onto piping, move pin to secure both the piping and binding to the quilt top, and add additional pins as needed. Sew from where you ended to where you began.
13. Evaluate corners, piping, and binding before cutting quilt top to binding edge.
14. Bring the binding fold to the back of the quilt and stitch in place by hand.

Santa Fe, 23" Square. Machine Pieced and Hand Quilted by Author.

SANTA FE

I have always loved quilts using diamond shapes, and the LeMoyne Star block is a favorite. This quilt combines whole and half 3" Morning Star blocks with half 6" Lone Stars. These blocks are essentially LeMoyne Stars that have been fragmented and set on point with a split alternate block and side triangle. Splitting the alternate block and adding half stars adds detail.

Using the same mauve in the side triangle area anchors and unites the quilt.

A simple mitered border of four multiple strips of fabric surrounds the stars. The very narrow border adds just a touch of lightness and brightness to the outside. The texture created by the quilting adds to their beauty and completes the quilt.

- Quilt Size: 23" square
- Block Size: 3" and 6" finished
- Techniques Used: Strip piecing, templates, Y-seams

Fabric Requirements:

- Stars: about ½ yard total, but use lots of ⅛-yard pieces of different colors and shades to make the quilt more interesting
- 3" Whole Star Background: ⅛-yard pieces of lots of choices
- Unifying Fabric, background of both the half 3" and 6" stars, and border: ½ yard
- Alternate Blocks: 5" squares of several different fabrics
- Borders: ⅓ yard for the navy borders, ⅛ yard for the very narrow border (accent color)
- Binding: 110" of ¾" wide straight grain, single fold
- Backing: 27" square
- Batting: 27" square

3" Morning Star

The Morning Star block is a basic LeMoyne Star, fragmented or fractured from eight diamonds into thirty-two diamonds. This star is drafted from a circle, rather than a grid of equal divisions across and down, and has three shapes and forty pieces (thirty-two diamonds, four squares and four triangles). There are two design elements: the background, and the star or diamonds. Think of the large diamond shape that holds the four small diamonds as a four-patch on a slant. You will assemble them in that way, by sewing strips, and then cutting and sewing segments together.

The diamond (four-patch on a slant) is deliberately oversized. A template is used to fine-cut the diamond to the appropriate size. Open, well-pressed, and trimmed seams are most important to the technical success of this block. You need eight of these diamonds joined with four corners and four side triangles of background to complete one whole 3" Morning Star. To begin, choose three star fabrics and one background fabric.

Diamonds

Tone-on-tone, low activity, quiet fabric works well in the small diamond area. There are three circular positions of color. Position 1 congregates in the center and creates a very small LeMoyne Star. The more solid your fabric, the more revealing; the busier the fabric, the more forgiving. Squint at the project quilt and no-

tice that some of the inner stars are light, some dark, some are subtle and not as clearly defined. This relates to the value of Fabric 2, not what color it is. Value (light, medium, dark) develops design.

Note: The thread color should be well blended to Fabric 1. The center joins eight points together, and the opportunity for thread to show is increased.

Position 2 is dominant and creates a continuous circle around the middle of the star. Position 3 is the star tips. They touch the background fabric, so you must create contrast between the background and tips to have them show.

Note: Before the diamond is sewn, while it is still in two segments, you can reposition them to create different arrangements.

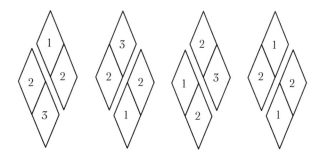

Background

The background shapes are the largest pieces and can use the busier, large-scaled fabrics. Templates will allow for specific positioning, so working with directional fabrics in the background area is easily accomplished and very effective.

Note: You can interview background fabric by positioning a diamond (or just two slices positioned like a diamond, but not sewn) on different background choices and then placing the taped mirrors around the diamond. Positioning the mirror in around the diamond edges allows you to see the complete star. Interview a variety of prints, colors, and values for the background position.

Y-Seam or Inset Seam Construction

This star requires Y-Seam or Inset Seam construction. This kind of sewing is needed when three seams meet in one place and it becomes necessary to leave the seam allowance free to accomplish a flat, smooth intersection. You will sew straight, either from an outside edge to a dot and backstitch, or from the center edge to a dot and backstitch, or from dot to dot and backstitch. This kind of sewing is choppy and slower, but it is not difficult. Just resign yourself to the fact that this is not a fast chain-piecing kind of star.

The holes punched in the templates allow you to make dots on the fabric. The dots indicate the seam allowance area. If you stitch just one thread into the seam allowance, you create a pucker. I have found that if you stop sewing just before entering the dot and backstitch, it works successfully every time. Sometimes I dial the stitch length smaller as I approach the dot, but never sew into the dot. Pinning and matching dots not only helps to rest one fabric onto another, it helps to align edges and identify the sewing path.

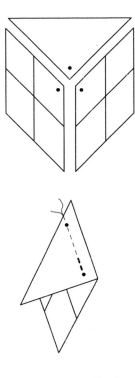

One Whole 3" Morning Star—Make 12

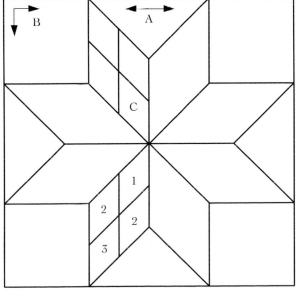

Block Diagram

1. Make accurate templates for Shapes A, B, and C from the block diagram, adding ¼" seam allowance on all sides. Transfer all placement lines and identifying information on each template, punching holes at each intersection. Refer to Templates, page 25.

   Shape A and B: Wait until after the diamonds are formed to select and cut four each from background fabric.

   Shape C is the large whole diamond shape that holds four smaller diamonds inside it.

2. Decide on star Fabrics 1, 2, and 3. Cut one 1" x 16" straight grain strip from Fabrics 1 and 3. Cut two 1" x 16" straight grain strips from Fabric 2.

   Note: All diamond seams will be pressed open.

3. Sew strips of Fabric 1 and 2 together lengthwise, press stitches, finger-press seam open, press with iron, trim both sides. How well you sew and press at the very beginning will affect the quality of the finished block. Sew Fabric 2 and 3 together similarly.

   Note: Be attentive to thread color and stitch length!

4. With fabric right side up, develop a 45° angle on the end of each strip unit as illustrated and cut eight 1" slices from each strip unit.

Note: To maintain the correct angle, always keep the 45° line of the ruler on the seam and the 1" line of the ruler on the edge of the fabric. If it becomes difficult to keep both lines positioned properly, it simply means the angle is tipped off and needs to be reestablished.

5. Now is when you can arrange two slices (one from each strip unit) into a diamond and place it on different prints, colors, and values to interview backgrounds. Place the taped mirrors around one diamond and you will see what the entire star will look like. Reposition the slices to develop different arrangements of color. See illustration on page 102. Determine which orientation you want and look at it one more time in the mirrors.

6. Pick up two slices, one from each strip unit, and form the diamond. Place the two slices right sides together, being aware of what edges will get sewn.

   Note: It's very important that you sew the correct edges, or the color and/or fabric will be out of position. Focus on and prepare one diamond at a time for sewing.

7. To match the intersection, keep the slices paired; make a mark $\frac{1}{4}$" down from the correct edge on one seam. Turn the pair over and mark similarly on the second slice. Using a positioning pin, pin through the mark on the open seam of the slice facing you and into the mark and open seam of the other slice. The position pin will help rest one slice onto another and align the edges. Place a pin at each end. Place an additional pin, positioned as illustrated, just next to the position pin and then remove the position pin. Remember, the position pin does not secure the intersection. Some machines take on pins differently, thus the three pin placements.

   Note: The pin must travel through the thread area of the open seam, not through any fabric.

8. Sew the slices together, sewing across the mark. You can also draw a $\frac{1}{4}$" sewing line all the way across, although you must still match the center seam with the position pin.

   If you are having a problem matching the center intersection, it could only be that you need improvement in one or more of the following:

   a. *Did not match both marks with pin accurately.*
   b. *Did not sew over mark (maybe you sewed just above or just below).*
   c. *Pin placement might need to be changed.*
   d. *Pin not positioned through the thread area of the open seam.*

9. When the intersection is matched, press the stitches, open the seam with your hands, press with the iron. Evaluate and trim the seams. Repeat for the remaining seven diamonds.

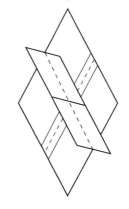

10. The diamonds you have created are oversized and need to be cut down to assemble the block. Place Template C face up on the right side of one of the oversized diamonds, aligning center and lines on template with intersection and seams on diamond. Trace around the template very carefully; do not mark the dots on the right side of the fabric. Cut out the diamond shape, cutting the line off. Turn the diamond over and place the template face down on the wrong side of the diamond and mark dots on the fabric through the punched holes of your template. Use a marking tool that does not bleed into your fabric and show on the right side. Repeat for the remaining seven diamonds. They are now the size needed to assemble the star.

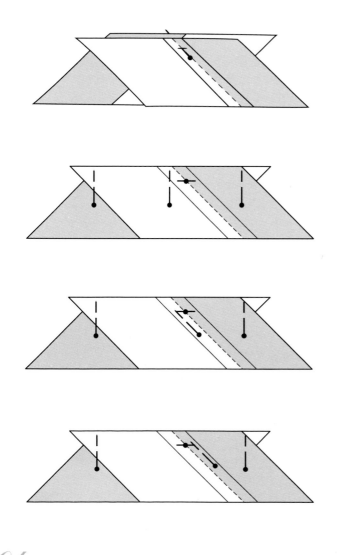

Note: I cut out the shape and mark the dots in two steps because I can see more clearly from the right side to position the template lines to seam lines to get a more accurate tracing of the shape. I then turn the diamond over to mark the dots. If you can see clearly from the wrong side, you can trace the shape and mark dots in one step.

11. Cut out the background fabric from Shapes A and B and lay out the block. Be sure diamonds are positioned correctly and the color placement is where you want it.

12. Make four ACC units. Position your work to look just like the illustrations. Pin the triangle to the diamond by inserting pins into appropriate dots on both pieces to help position and align edges of both pieces and to rest them on one another. Secure pins and sew in the direction of the arrows, from the outer edge almost to the dot, and backstitch. Add the second diamond to the triangle similarly. To sew from the edge to the dot both times, sew with the diamond on top once and then the triangle on top once. Now position the two diamonds right sides together, pin at the two dots, and align and pin the seam in the center of the diamond as well. Sew from the center edge almost to the dot and backstitch. Press the diamond seam open, press the triangle seams toward the diamonds. Arrange and finger-press before using the iron and handle carefully, as the diamond edges are bias and could stretch. Trim both sides of the open seam and the triangle seams. Repeat for the remaining three ACC units.

Center

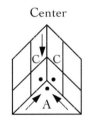

13. Sew a B square to the right side of each ACC unit. Sew from the outside edge almost to the dot and backstitch. Do not press or trim; lay out block in front of you again.

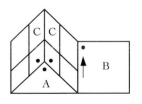

14. Now join two ABCC units together, sewing from the outside edge almost to the dot and backstitch. Then sew diamonds together from center edge almost to the dot and backstitch, matching the seam in the middle. Press diamond seam open, press square seams toward square. Trim only the diamond seam at this time. The square seams will be trimmed when the block is complete. Repeat for remaining two ABCC units.

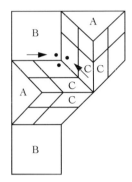

Note: Evaluate the two halves at the center point to be sure you have created a sharp V or point on both. The whole star center will only be as good as the two halves!

15. Sew the two halves of the star together from the outside edge almost to the dot and backstitch. Sew the long center seam last, matching and pinning dots, the center, and the two points on either side of center. Use a positioning pin to align the center points first.

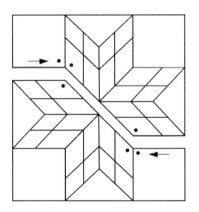

Note: To begin sewing, slide your sewing machine needle in front of the pin and into the fabric, hold the threads, and take a couple of stitches and backstitch. Continue sewing across the center seam, keeping the seam allowances smooth on the bottom. Sew slowly, compressing the fabric in front of the needle with a seam ripper or stiletto to create a groove for the needle to sew into. Sew almost to the dot and backstitch.

16. Evaluate the star for a matched center and well-shaped diamonds, as well as measuring 3½" square, or reasonably so. If all is well, open and press the center seam, press the square seams toward the squares, and trim. Star is complete. Make 11 more.

Note: The multicolored, scrappy look in two of the stars is accomplished by using slices from many different strip units. You could use two fabrics for a star and arrange a checkerboard look, or use up to 32 different fabrics; the choices are limitless!

Half 3" Morning Star—Make 3

1. Cutting instructions makes one half 3" Morning Star.
   Shape A: Cut four from background
   Shape B: Cut one from background
   Shape C: Make four C diamonds from chosen fabrics as described in the 3" whole Morning Star.

2. Lay out the half star as illustrated and make any changes necessary.

Note: The pressing and trimming procedure is the same as the whole Morning Star. All diamond seams are pressed opened, the square seams are pressed toward the square, the triangle seams are pressed toward the diamonds.

3. Make two ACC units as described in Whole 3" Morning Star, step 12, page 105.

4. Add a B square to the right side of one ACC unit. Sew from edge to dot and backstitch.

5. Add an A triangle to the right side of one ACC unit. Sew from edge to edge.

6. Join the ACCB and ACCA units as illustrated. Sew from edge to dot and backstitch.

7. Add an A triangle as illustrated. Sew from edge to edge.

8. Repeat for two more halves.

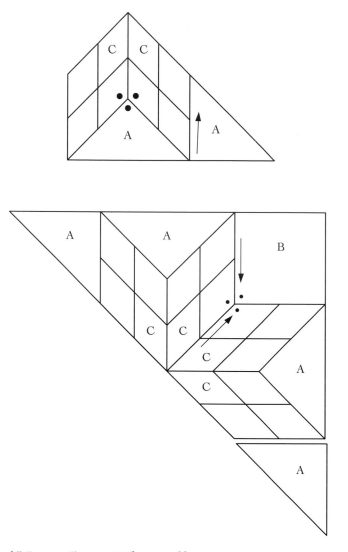

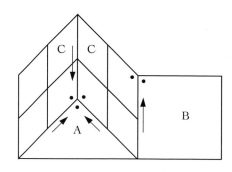

6" Lone Star—Make 2 Half Stars

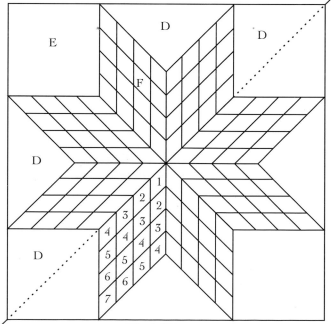

Block Diagram

Each large diamond of the 6" Lone Star holds sixteen small diamonds of the same size as the ones used in the 3" Morning Star. Instead of creating one four-patch on slant, you will create four four-patches on slant and join them to create each large diamond. The size of the block doubles to 6". The diamond size in both blocks is the same; only A and B background shapes change.

The Lone Star has seven circular positions of color to play with. When choosing fabric and color, keep in mind the following:

- Position 1 will create a small LeMoyne star in the center.
- Position 4 makes a prominent circle.
- Position 7 is the tip and should contrast with the background fabric.

Note: The unifying fabric (mauve) is used in the background of all the half stars.

1. Make templates for Shape D triangle and Shape E square. See Templates on page 25.

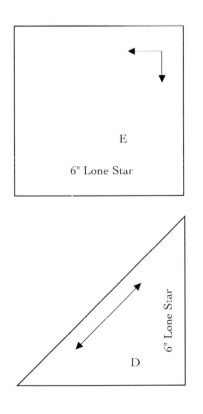

E

6" Lone Star

6" Lone Star

D

2. Cutting instructions makes both halves.
   Shape D: Cut eight from background fabric (four for each half).
   Shape E: Cut two from background fabric (one for each half).
3. Shape F: Make eight. Each is created from four Shape C's from the 3" Morning Star. Join the four Shape C's like you would assemble a four-patch,

matching all intersections and creating well shaped diamonds. Open the seams, press well and trim seams. It is extremely important to control the bulk and keep the star flat.

4. Cut 1" x 16" straight grain strips of the following: one strip each of Fabrics 1 and 7, two strips each of Fabrics 2 and 6, three strips each of Fabrics 3 and 5, and four strips of Fabric 4.

Note: The number of strips cut is determined by how many times that fabric appears in the large Shape F diamond.

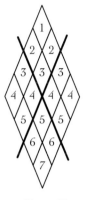

Shape F

5. Sew appropriate strips together, open the seam, press, and trim. With fabric right side up, develop a 45° angle on all the two-strip units and cut eight 1" slices from each as you did in the 3" star, maintaining an accurate angle.

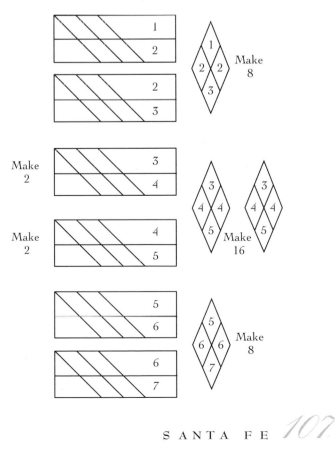

6. Sew the appropriate slices together, matching the center intersection as you did for the 3" star, open the seam, press, and trim.

7. Use the Shape C template (from 3" Morning Star)on the 32 four-diamond units, being sure to mark the dots on the wrong side of the fabric.

8. Referring to the illustration, assemble four Shape C's together, match intersections, open seams, steam press, and trim carefully. Repeat seven times.

Note: You will need to make a mark ¹/₄" down from correct edges on the seam as a guide for matching the intersections, as described in the 3" star.

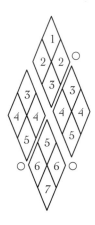

9. Arrange four large F diamonds with one E square and four D triangles and assemble, press, and trim, as described in the half 3" Morning Star (page 106).

10. Repeat for the second half. All the whole stars and half stars are now complete.

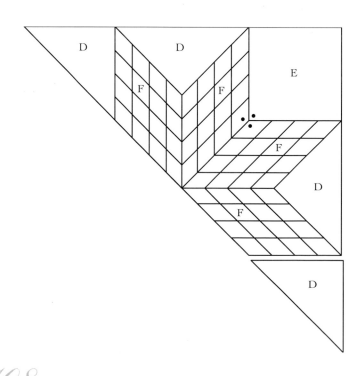

Alternate Blocks—Make 10

This area is simply a 3" square that is split diagonally into two triangles. In the project quilt nine of the G triangles, and all of the H triangles, are from the unifying fabric.

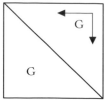

Shape G: Cut ten 3⁷/₈" squares of chosen fabric, cut in half diagonally. This keeps straight grain on the two short sides of the triangle.

Side Triangles—Need 9

Shape H and G are the same size and shape, but the grain placement is different.

Shape H: Cut three 5¹/₂" squares of chosen fabrics, cut into quarters diagonally. This keeps the straight grain on the longest side of the triangle.

Quilt Assembly

1. Lay out the stars, half stars, alternate block triangles, and side triangles to form the quilt top. Feel free to change and reposition the blocks and triangles; this is the fun part. Now is a good time to have a reducing glass and an instant camera. This quilt changes a lot depending on where values are placed and whether the seam in the alternate block is vertical or horizontal. Have fun experimenting.

2. When you are satisfied with the placement of all the elements, you are ready to sew the interior of the quilt together. First sew the G triangles to form squares. Place the triangles right sides together, matching all three edges. Sew across the bias edge with an accurate ¹/₄" seam allowance. Press the stitches, then open to a square and press the seam allowance in one direction. Do one GG square at a time to keep the color placement accurate.

3. Assemble the quilt top as illustrated. Match and pin intersections, press and trim seams carefully. Good pressing skills are the key to this quilt. Arrows indicate seam direction. Open seams are indicated by a circle.

Borders

This quilt has four borders. In the project quilt, Borders 1 and 4 are the same fabric, a deep, dark value. Border 2 is very narrow and brings some brightness to the outside, and Border 3 is the same unifying fabric.

• Border 1: Cut four 27" x ⁷/₈" strips from navy fabric.

- Border 2: Cut four 27" x 1¼" strips from accent fabric.
- Border 3: Cut four 27" x 2" strips from unifying fabric.
- Border 4: Cut four 27" x 2½" strips from navy fabric

Note: It helps significantly to arrange and press the borders strips carefully, right sides together, before sewing.

1. Sew Border 1 to Border 2 with a ¼" seam allowance, press stitches, trim the seam allowance to an accurate ⅛" with a ruler and rotary cutter or scissors, press seam allowance toward Border 2.
2. Sew Border 3 to Border 1–2, with 1–2 on top. Align raw edges of borders and sew just along the cut edge of the just-trimmed seam allowance. You are now creating the very narrow accent border. How straight you cut and sew determines the success of the border.

3. Press stitches, trim seam allowance to within ¼" of the last line of stitching, press seam allowance toward Border 3.
4. Sew Border 4 to Border 1–2–3, with 1–2–3 on top, using a ¼" seam allowance. Press stitches, press seam allowance toward Border 4.
5. Repeat for the remaining three border units. Sew borders to quilt top starting and stopping at ¼" from the edge and backstitch. Refer to Mitering Corners by Hand on page 34. Your quilt top is complete.

Finishing

Mark quilting lines, if applicable, baste, and quilt. Bind using ¾" wide straight grain single fold binding applied with a ⅛" seam allowance.

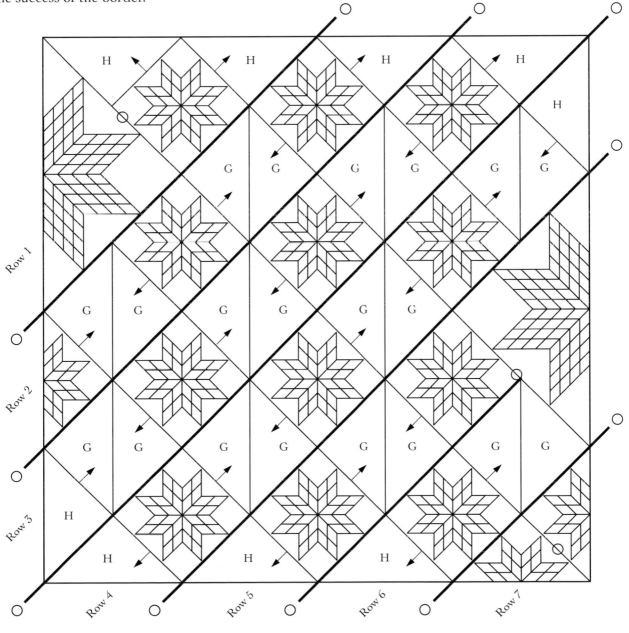

BIBLIOGRAPHY

Anthony, Catherine H. *Sampler Supreme*, Santa Clara, California: Leone Publishing Co., 1983.

Beyer, Jinny. *Patchwork Patterns*, McLean, Virginia: EPM Publications, 1979.

Dietrich, Mimi. *Happy Endings*, Bothell, Washington: That Patchwork Place, 1987.

Hargrave, Harriet. *Heirloom Machine Quilting*, Lafayette, California: C&T Publishing, 1995.

Johnson-Srebro, Nancy. *Miniature to Masterpiece*, Columbia Crossroads, Pennsylvania: RCW Publishing Co., 1990.

McCloskey, Marsha. *Lessons in Machine Piecing*, Bothell, Washington: That Patchwork Place, 1990.

McClun, Diana, and Laura Nownes. *Quilts Galore!*, San Francisco: The Quilt Digest Press, 1990.

McClun, Diana, and Laura Nownes. *Quilts, Quilts, Quilts*, San Francisco: The Quilt Digest Press, 1988.

Rodgers, Sue H. *Trapunto*, Wheatridge, Colorado: Moon Over The Mountain Publishing Co., 1990.

Schaefer, Becky. *Working in Miniature*, Lafayette, California: C&T Publishing, 1987.

Thomas, Donna Lynn. *Small Talk*, Bothell, Washington: That Patchwork Place, 1991.

SOURCES

The Cotton Club
P.O. Box 2263
Boise, ID 83701
(208) 345–5567
$1/16$" hole punch

The Cotton Patch
1025 Brown Avenue
Lafayette, CA 94549
(800) 835-4418
(510) 284-1177
$1/16$" hole punch, fabric, quilting supplies, and books

OTHER FINE BOOKS
FROM C&T PUBLISHING

For more information write for a free catalog from

C&T Publishing ◆ P.O. Box 1456 ◆ Lafayette, CA 94549 ◆ (800) 284-1114

ABOUT THE AUTHOR

Photo by Joe Collins.

Sally Collins grew up in Trenton, Michigan, and moved to California in 1975. She took her first quilting class in 1978 and found the joy that comes with putting in the stitch. Her immediate and continual love and interest was in the process of quiltmaking, the doing. This interest in attention to detail led Sally to what she describes as small scale quiltmaking. She dreams, designs, and colors in full size and then technically translates that image into a scale of her own choosing. She loves the challenge, both technically and creatively, of designing large and working small. Through this book she hopes to introduce quiltmakers to her perspective on quiltmaking and perhaps persuade you to try it.

Sally spends her time traveling across the country sharing quilts and teaching workshops, managing her own pattern company, Special Treasures, and enjoying life with her husband Joe, son Sean, daughter-in-law Evelyn, and granddaughter Kaylin.

Workshop and lecture inquiries may be sent directly to Sally Collins at 1640 Fieldgate Lane, Walnut Creek, California, 94595.